Applying Behavioural Science to the Private Sector

Helena Rubinstein

Applying Behavioural Science to the Private Sector

Decoding What People Say and What They Do

Helena Rubinstein
Innovia Technology Ltd
Cambridge, UK

ISBN 978-3-030-01697-5   ISBN 978-3-030-01698-2   (eBook)
https://doi.org/10.1007/978-3-030-01698-2

Library of Congress Control Number: 2018958001

Cover illustration: © Melisa Hasan

This Palgrave Pivot imprint is published by the registered company Springer Nature
Switzerland AG
The registered company address is: Gewerbestrasse 11, 6330 Cham, Switzerland

To Brian, Ilana and Nadia

PREFACE

The idea for this book came from a discussion with a Principal Scientist and Research Fellow at a global pharmaceutical company. He told me that his organisation might benefit from using behavioural science, but he didn't know where to start. *"I have heard about nudging. Is that the same as behavioural science? I don't know enough about it or how to find someone who is really good at it. I've received lots of emails from people who claim they do behavioural science but how do I know what is good or what is right for us?"*

He was making a point I had heard many times. Behavioural science has become unusually high profile and many businesses are exploring how to use it. However, it is a relatively new discipline and there are not many guides for how to use it well in a commercial setting.

At Innovia Technology, where I manage a team of behavioural scientists, we have been working with global corporations on their behavioural challenges for many years. The team comprises practitioners from across the psychological sciences including social psychologists, health psychologists, experimental psychologists, cognitive neuroscientists, behavioural economists, public health specialists, and sports psychologists. We all come from an academic background and have been applying academic theory in a way that is well-suited to the faster pace of the commercial sector to design better products, services and interventions.

This book is the result of these experiences. It is intended to help students know how to use behavioural science theory and apply it in business, and help managers know how and when to use behavioural science, as well as overcome the challenges to incorporating it in their businesses.

People believe that they understand human behaviour because they are human. However, it's almost impossible to intuitively know how people will behave. People say one thing and do another. It is hard to predict human behaviour and even harder to change it, but if we use a structured and rigorous approach, we can get better at understanding why people don't always do what they say they do.

Cambridge, UK   Helena Rubinstein

ACKNOWLEDGMENTS

I'd like to thank my colleagues at Innovia for their support and comments while I was writing this book. In particular, Dr Geraint Davies read and improved early drafts of every chapter and Dr Guen Bradbury gave detailed and invaluable advice to improve readability. In addition, I would like to thank those colleagues who contributed or were interviewed including Dr Colin Ager, Dr Emma Bertenshaw, Hannah Burt, Dr Marie Buda, Dr Helen Clubb, Dr Tim Goldrein, Gabriel Greening, Dr Caroline Hagerman, Dr Alex Hellawell, Glenn Le Faou, Dr Alastair McGregor, Dr Fiona McMaster, Dr Katie Morton, Andy Milton, Dr Shreyas Mukund, Kora Muscat, Arron Rodrigues, Ben Rose, Dr Julian Scarfe, James Salisbury, and Dr Rob Wilkinson.

I am also grateful to my clients for allowing me to work on so many fascinating challenges. I am especially indebted to Heather Figallo at Southwest Airlines and Allie Kelly at The Ray for their helpful comments on the case studies.

ABOUT THE BOOK

This book is divided into two parts. Part I focuses on the theory and principles of behavioural science and Part II describes how this theory can effectively be put into practice in commercial organisations. Case studies are used to illustrate major themes.

The aim of Part I is to describe the *underlying theory and principles* behind the discipline. I outline the history of behavioural science, discuss why behaviour is hard to predict, and explain how behavioural scientists use theories and models of behaviour. In the last chapter of this section, I show a process for how theory is applied to design products, services and interventions.

Part II is about *practice*. Much of this section is based on case studies or interviews with practitioners. I discuss the challenges of integrating behavioural science into an established organisation and suggest how and why to use behavioural science in multidisciplinary teams. In Chap. 7, I use a case study to show how the process described in Part I was applied to improve the boarding experience at the gate for Southwest Airlines. I also consider the potential for misuse of behavioural science and suggest ethical guidelines that could be used in the private sector. Finally, I discuss the value of applying behavioural science to business and propose how best to realise its potential.

Contents

About the Author

Helena Rubinstein is Head of Behavioural Science and leads the Strategic Advisory Group at Innovia Technology, an innovation consultancy based in Cambridge, UK. Her academic background is in social psychology and she has lectured at the University of Cambridge on the application of social psychology to social issues and on the psychology of ageing. She has also conducted research in the field of health psychology.

Helena has extensive commercial experience and has held senior positions in advertising and communications. She was managing director of the global brand consultancy for Leo Burnett and a partner at Brunswick Group.

She is married with two children and lives in Cambridge.

LIST OF FIGURES

LIST OF BOXES

PART I

Theory and Principles of Behavioural Science

This section focuses on the theory of behavioural science and its relevance to commercial issues. It describes the basic principles and the main theories that underpin behavioural science.

The aim is to help readers to understand what behaviour is, how behavioural scientists describe and model behaviour, and how to use this knowledge to improve research, product and service development, and intervention design.

Chapter 1 provides an overview of behavioural science. It describes how the discipline of behavioural science developed from ideas emerging from social and health psychology, how these ideas challenged classical economic theory, and how they have been transferred, and successfully used by policy makers. It explores the main principles of nudge theory and suggests that there is more to behavioural science than 'nudging'. The chapter concludes that businesses would benefit from applying the scientific method of behavioural science in the commercial sector, if they can overcome five major challenges to its implementation.

Chapter 2 focusses on the difficulty of predicting behaviour, explains the intention–behaviour gap, and explores why existing market research methods are not good enough at predicting behaviour. Conventional methods often fail to yield useful information because the data collected is often poor quality, data is confused with insight, the research fails to focus on the factors that drive behaviour, and the research is done to confirm existing biases rather than to prove or refute behavioural hypotheses. This chapter describes the barriers that prevent businesses developing a deeper understanding of consumer behaviour. It explains why businesses need better research tools and methods that apply the principles of behavioural science if they are to design products and services that are intuitive to use and that people want. It clarifies the need for a good theoretical framework to allow researchers to find out what people really do, not what they say they do.

Chapter 3 describes the science behind behaviour and why theories and models are useful. They provide focus, help to cut through complexity, and guide decisions about what products, services and interventions to design and develop. It argues that too many businesses focus on changing attitudes and beliefs rather than on the behaviours themselves. Without a good theory or model of behaviour, companies do not know what activities to observe, or what is really important in influencing behaviour. It discusses what makes a good theory or model of behaviour and how organisations can use and develop models to understand specific challenges. It illustrates how theories, such as the COM-B and the Unified Theory of Acceptance and Use of Technology Model, benefit decision-making and how they can be used in practice.

Chapter 4 explores the application of theory to intervention design and explains why a structured approach is vital. It outlines a five-step process that can be applied in business, starting with defining the desired behavioural outcome, taking the reader through approaches for doing a behavioural diagnostic, prioritising the influences on behaviour, identifying suitable behaviour-change techniques, ideating products, services and interventions and prioritising them, and ends with how to test and evaluate them. It describes how a structured approach helps to refine a large number of options down to a small number of intervention ideas that have a good probability of success. It concludes that using a systematic process, which is grounded in evidence and theory, results in solutions that are more likely to be effective *and* acceptable to the consumer.

CHAPTER 1

An Overview of Behavioural Science

Why Businesses Don't Use It and Why They Should

Abstract This chapter focuses on how the discipline of behavioural science developed from ideas emerging from social and health psychology, how these ideas challenged classical economic theory, and how they have been transferred, and successfully used by policy makers. Rubinstein explores the main principles of nudge theory and suggests that there is more to behavioural science than 'nudging'. She concludes that businesses would benefit from applying the scientific method of behavioural science in the commercial sector, if they can overcome five major challenges to its implementation.

Keywords Behavioural science • Nudge theory • Scientific method

How good are you at driving?

Be honest—how good are your driving skills *really?*

Peoples' sense of their own driving ability is deeply embedded. Most will tell you that they are 'above average'. Even if you tell them that, of course, they can't *all* be above average, they'll say "yeah, but I *am* above average".

This is relevant if you are trying to design systems to help people to drive better, and more safely. If you ask a person to describe her

© The Author(s) 2018

H. Rubinstein, *Applying Behavioural Science to the Private Sector,*

https://doi.org/10.1007/978-3-030-01698-2_1

actions while, for example, merging from a smaller road onto a big one, she will probably describe a standard 'textbook' manoeuvre. She won't tell you what happens when the phone rings, when she is distracted by her children in the back, when she is late for work, tired, or gripped by road rage. For the more experienced drivers, many driving behaviours have become habitual and automatic, so people aren't really aware of what they are doing or thinking while driving. And the way we ask questions about driving doesn't help. We tend to ask about driving behaviour as if everyone is always rational and we fail to take account of the social and emotional factors that influence what we do.

This was the problem facing the team at Innovia Technology when they were designing novel systems to improve safety on the road. So, how did the team face these challenges? The narrative below summarises some of their thinking and processes.

Glenn arrived at the meeting late. *"Sorry, the traffic is always terrible when it's been raining. There was a collision. People just don't realise they need to change their driving behaviour when the conditions change."*

"You should know," Marie, the psychologist, commented. *"You're the transport designer! Anyway, you've arrived at just the right moment—we're talking about the solutions to prevent road accidents for The Ray."*

The Ray is a not-for-profit organisation that manages 18 miles of highway in Georgia that is working to make roads greener and safer. Its mission is 'Zero Carbon, Zero Waste, Zero Death'. The Ray developed as a result of an epiphany by the founder of Interface, Inc, Ray C. Anderson. He had grown the business into the world's largest manufacturer of modular carpets, but realised that his company, and all of business and industry, was causing tremendous environmental damage. Furthermore, he recognised that only businesses like his were sufficiently large, capitalised, and organised to solve global environmental challenges. In 1994, he committed to making his organisation sustainable, so that it could eventually operate with no harm to the biosphere. For the remaining 17 years of his life, he proved that a company's authentic commitment to environmental sustainability was not only morally right: it was also remarkably profitable. Today, The Ray describes itself as 'a living lab for innovative ideas and technologies that can set a new standard for roadways around the world and prove that ambitious goals are within our reach'.

This meeting at Innovia was focused on how to improve driving safety.

Marie had been sifting through piles of statistics and reports on driving behaviour. *"Did you know that 95% of accidents are caused by drivers themselves and 40% are rear-end collisions? Most crashes occur because people don't pay attention to the road—they look but they don't see, or they only see what they expect to see."*

The client relationship manager, Andy, who was a physicist, had been looking at all the solutions that had been tried previously. *"There are so many ways of approaching this problem—signage, traffic calming, vehicle tracking, and more. And there's so much data! How do we know where to focus?"*

"Signs and signals don't always help," said Marie. *"Only about 15% of people's attention is given to road signs. If you show people ten signs while driving, they only recall seeing one of them! And when you increase the number of signs, you actually lull people into a false sense of security, so they pay even less attention"*

"So, where should we focus?" asked Glenn.

"I've been looking at the psychology of driving behaviour," said Marie. *"There are several behavioural models we could use to understand the way in which drivers do, (or don't) make good decisions. I think the most useful one here would be the Theory of Planned Behaviour. Let's start with this. We might need to modify as we get new data, but it will help us to decide what is important initially."*

Over the next few weeks, the team investigated the types of accidents that were happening, explored why they were happening, and analysed the psychology of drivers. The behavioural model helped the group to identify effective ways to change driving behaviour.

A few weeks later, the team was reviewing the findings.

Marie started the conversation. *"The key to increasing safety is to keep people alert. If they have too little to do, they don't pay attention.*

Most drivers think they are better than average—they don't like to be told what to do even if it is for their own good. Anything we create needs to fit with the driver's own view of the situation, otherwise drivers won't accept it.".

"Different drivers make mistakes for different reasons—some are overconfident, some are nervous. We need to address all of these reasons," Andy added.

Glenn agreed. *"We've looked at lots of different ideas and have come up with a range of possible solutions. The strongest idea has never been done before, but it fits the behavioural model well and looks technically very promising. It involves using solar-powered LED road studs to give subtle cues to the driver to help them drive more safely. I think this is a really powerful option."*

And he was right. The team developed a range of ways in which the solar-powered studs could communicate with road users. The studs could flash at different speeds to encourage people to slow down or speed up, or they could turn red to indicate when a driver was too close to the car in front.

Fig. 1.1 Schematic of speed-control pulsing and gradated warning used to test comprehensibility and usefulness of solar-powered road studs. Source: Innovia Technology

To test this idea, the team built a series of 3D simulations from the driver's perspective (Fig. 1.1.) and tested them with different types of drivers, ranging from the novice to the experienced, and from the risk-averse to the risk-takers. During the tests, people were asked what they thought the lights meant and what they would do as a result. The responses were positive: people found the road stud signals intuitive and thought that they would be useful on the road to improve their driving behaviour.

In 2017, The Ray made prototypes of the studs and applied for patents. In 2018, the solar-powered road stud was a finalist for Fast Company's World-Changing Ideas Awards, which reward concepts and products that make the world better. The Ray continues to explore and develop new technologies to make highways sustainable and safer.

*   *   *

So, what does this story tell us about using behavioural science? One, a validated behavioural model helps to make sense of a lot of data and to know where to focus solutions. Two, understanding the decision-making process (how drivers decide to do what they do) is vital. And three, testing and evaluating interventions is critical to ensure that solutions are acceptable, feasible and effective.

Let's look at these in a bit more detail. A behavioural model is one that has been created by behavioural scientists because they think it might be a useful way of explaining why people do what they do. A validated behavioural model has been tested by behavioural scientists with a huge amount of data—and they can see whether the model predicts accurately how people behave. So, using a proven model in a new situation (such as in the car, on the road) helped Innovia to work out what was important and what we should ignore.

Understanding the decision-making process is important because it helps us to see which factors matter most in influencing behaviour and allows us to ignore those that are unimportant. It means that we know when and how to target our interventions to change behaviour most effectively.

And finally, experimental approaches with real people in real or simulated situations helps us to work out whether our solutions have the potential to change behaviour in context. Context is critical. While models of behaviour are quite robust, due to sheer complexity of human nature, they *always* need to be tested because we may see different results in different contexts.

So, it's clear that we can use behavioural science to better understand what people need and to create solutions that deliver what they need. However, changing behaviour is rarely easy. This is why it is most effectively achieved by people who understand the underlying principles, can select the most appropriate model, and can interpret the data in light of that model. These are the skills of behavioural scientists.

1.1   How Did Behavioural Science Develop?

Behavioural science is seen as a relatively new discipline, but it's been around for a long time. It's just gone by a few different names. Aspects of the systematic study of human behaviour, individually and with each other, arise from social and health psychology, anthropology, sociology, and economics.

Human behaviour is complex. Unlike the physical behaviour of objects, human behaviour does not follow reliable, predictable laws. It is prone to change from day to day and even from moment to moment (West, 2015). The American Psychological Association defines behaviour as "anything a person does in response to internal or external events". Human behaviour is influenced by a very large number of factors, often acting simultaneously. These factors include our personal traits (including our motives and our attitudes and beliefs); the situations we find ourselves in at any given moment; the behaviour of other people; and our physical and social environments.

Unsurprisingly, these multiple influences make it very hard to predict what people will actually do. Let's take someone who really wants to lose weight. This person decides to stop eating chocolate and pastries, and confidently declares his ambition to his friends, family, and colleagues. However, regardless of his good intentions, he will find it hard to resist celebrating his friend's birthday with a piece of cake, he'll struggle to resist a piece of dessert when he's feeling a bit down, and he may find himself buying a chocolate bar at the garage without even thinking about it. Good intentions are often not enough to change behaviour in all situations, in part because people aren't aware of influences that subconsciously affect them.

Although it's hard to make consistently accurate predictions about people's behaviour, many people have tried to analyse behaviour systematically. From this, we see that while human behaviour can seem to be erratic and irrational, there are recognisable patterns that occur in different situations and under different influences. These systematic reviews and assessments of behaviour have come from different fields. Three of the most influential are from classical economics, from public policy, and from social and health psychology.

1.1.1 *From Classical Economics: Understanding Rationality and Irrationality*

Classical economics describes a theory of market economies as self-regulating systems, which are driven by production and exchange. However, the predictions from this theory are sometimes not supported by the evidence, and this is because people don't always behave rationally. Some of the key challenges to classical economic theory came from Herbert Simon, Amos Tversky and Daniel Kahneman, Cass Sunstein and Richard Thaler, and Dan Ariely. These led to the development of the field called behavioural economics. Let's look at these challengers in a bit more detail.

The economist **Herbert Simon** could be considered an early pioneer of behavioural science. He was a Nobel Prize winning economist, who believed that human behaviour could be studied scientifically. Among other things, he investigated behavioural decision-making and was most famous for his concepts of 'bounded rationality'[1] and 'satisficing'[2] (Simon, 1947). Unlike the economists of the day, Simon recognised that human beings do not make entirely rational decisions based on complete information. He suggested that people's ability to make decisions is limited by insufficient information. And even if people have all of the information

---

[1] Bounded rationality of individuals is limited by the information they have, the cognitive limitations of their minds, and the finite amount of time they have to make a decision.

[2] Satisficing is used to explain why individuals do not seek to maximise their benefit from a particular course of action (since they cannot assimilate and digest all the information that would be needed to do such a thing) and even if they could their minds would be unable to process it properly.

available, they lack the cognitive capacity to process it thoroughly. Therefore, because they can't work out how to 'maximise benefits,' they tend to just aim for 'good enough.' He said that human decision-making is made under conditions of uncertainty, is influenced by multiple factors, and that it is best understood as much by psychology as by economics.

Amos Tversky and Daniel Kahneman were social psychologists, but their work on decision-making challenged the classical economists' view that humans are rational decision-makers. Their research showed that humans don't analyse every decision in forensic detail. People make use of shortcuts, 'rules of thumb' or use 'heuristic biases' (simple, efficient rules), to make the decisions easier (Tversky & Kahneman, 1974). These cognitive biases are systematic (we are all prey to them) and are effective for making some decisions but not for others, so some decisions lead to outcomes that are not as good as expected.

Kahneman won the Nobel Prize in Economic Sciences in 2002 for Prospect Theory (Kahneman & Tversky, 1979); sadly Tversky had died before it was awarded. This highly influential (and much quoted) theory investigated people's attitudes to risk, and what characteristics of a situation made people 'risk-averse' or 'risk-seeking.' They found that the pain of losing is psychologically more powerful than the pleasure of gaining. 'Losses loom larger than gains.' In many instances, people would rather avoid a loss than gain a reward of similar, or even larger, logical value. This helps us frame information when trying to influence behaviour. We can stress the positives of performing a healthy behaviour: 'exercising more often will *reduce* the likelihood of becoming overweight.' This is gain-framing. Alternatively, we can stress the risks of not performing a healthy behaviour: 'exercising less often will *increase* the likelihood of becoming overweight'. This is loss framing. Prospect Theory tells us that in certain situations the second framing (loss framing) is likely to be more effective at changing behaviour.

There is no difference in the outcome described in these two statements, but there is a big difference in how people perceive them. If we frame the outcome negatively (that people are more likely to become overweight), more people engage with the improved behaviour because their fear of the negative outcome is greater than their desire for the positive one. People are influenced by the framing of decisions because of their inbuilt biases about potential losses and gains.

Kahneman argued that humans make irrational decisions because they use two systems of thinking in the brain: System 1 and System 2

(Kahneman, 2012). System 1 thinking is fast, automatic and emotional whereas System 2 thinking is slow, effortful and calculating. People use both of these systems to form judgments. As System 2 thinking takes more effort, people tend to default to System 1 thinking if the decision is hard, if the decision needs to be made quickly, or if they are distracted. If System 1 thinking is applied to the wrong decisions, the decision seems irrational, and the outcome may be less than desirable.

Researchers have since identified dozens of heuristics and cognitive biases ("List of cognitive biases, Wikipedia" 2016). Although some decisions made with heuristics seem irrational and bizarre, actually heuristics are efficient for most situations, most of the time. That's why people use them. However, if we understand these systematic biases, we can then predict and influence human behaviour, and we'll discuss this further later.

Cass Sunstein and Richard Thaler took Kahneman and Tversky's ideas about framing, cognitive biases, and Systems 1 and 2, and built them into Nudge Theory. In their book Nudge: Improving Decisions about Health, Wealth and Happiness, they describe a nudge as 'any aspect of the choice architecture that alters people's behaviour in a predictable way without forbidding any options or significantly changing their economic incentives' (Sunstein & Thaler, 2009, p. 6). Sunstein, a legal scholar and Thaler, an economist, saw that Kahneman and Tversky's theories helped to explain why people often made poor economic choices. They preferred the idea of nudging people rather than coercing them. Unsurprisingly, this approach attracted a lot of interest, especially from US politicians and policy makers, because they liked the idea of a relatively inexpensive way to give people choice but still encourage them to do the right thing.

Some of the key ideas of nudge theory include:

- *choice architecture*—how people's decision-making is affected by how choices are presented to them
- *anchoring*—how people intuitively assess probabilities against an implicitly suggested reference point,
- *the availability heuristic*—how people assess risk based on how easily they can think of examples,
- *status quo bias*—how people prefer the current state of affairs and see any change from the baseline as a loss
- *loss aversion*—how people strongly prefer avoiding losses to acquiring gains

Sunstein and Thaler described several different types of nudges. They suggested that, by understanding these biases, it is possible to design solutions that will encourage people to make better choices and improve their lives.

Writing around the same time as Sunstein and Thaler, **Dan Ariely**, a psychologist, showed how human beings were predictably irrational (Ariely, 2009). He focussed on how financial decisions are made, and like Sunstein and Thaler, he discussed the biases that affect human decision-making. Many of his coined phrases have entered the popular vocabulary. People like products more if they've created or assembled them—he called that the 'IKEA effect'. People value an item more if they own it or have chosen it: they will pay more to keep something that they own than to get something that they don't own, even if they've only just purchased it or have no reason to be attached to it. This is known as the 'endowment effect'

These scientists and writers challenged the views of classical economists, setting the scene for the development of behavioural economics as a separate discipline. Their ideas influenced many thinkers, and some of those were involved in creating policy.

1.1.2   From Public Policy: Changing How People Receive Information

In 2009, US President Barack Obama named Cass Sunstein as head of the Office of Information and Regulatory Affairs (OIRA). Sunstein's goal was to make regulation more cost effective by reviewing regulation from many departments to ensure that the benefits justified the costs (Sunstein, 2012). He applied the principles from behavioural economics to improve the way people received government information.

Sunstein knew that people don't make rational economic choices, and he instead looked at changing the choice architecture to nudge people to make good decisions. His team applied the principles of nudge theory to a 'food pyramid' designed by the US Department of Agriculture, which aimed to encourage people to eat a healthy diet. The pyramid was very confusing. Instead, the team recommended a new graphic—MyPlate—that showed a plate divided into four segments (Fig. 1.2). Each quarter of the plate had a different food group: fruits and vegetables, grains and protein, and there was also a separate but smaller plate for dairy products. This simple graphic related directly to food and was far easier to understand.

Fig. 1.2   The MyPlate symbol: a reminder for use on food packaging to help people make healthy food choices. Source: United States Department of Agriculture

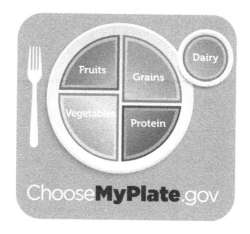

Sunstein applied these behavioural principles to a wide range of US government challenges ranging from the regulation and design of the 2009 CARD Act (Lunn, 2014, p. 27) to the regulations of food labelling (Lunn, 2014, p. 28). Nudge theory was explicitly used for the Credit Card Accountability Responsibility and Disclosure Act (CARD) which was designed to counter unfair practices by US credit card companies that took advantage of various well-known cognitive biases. For example, consumers pay insufficient attention to potential future costs (a bias known as hyperbolic discounting) and are too optimistic when assessing the likelihood of incurring fees (optimism bias). The CARD act tried to limit these behavioural biases by banning the hiding of fees and insisting that lenders supplied more helpful and timely information. Lenders were also mandated to include an explicit calculation on bills of the time and cost of making minimum payments each month to clear the bill and a similar calculation of repaying over 36 months. A recent analysis (Agarwal, Chomsisengphet, Mahoney, & Stroebel, 2015) estimated that the regulation of hidden fees saved consumers $21 billion per year and the nudge involving explicit calculations led to a significant impact on repayments.

During this time, the **Behavioural Insights Team** (BIT) was set up inside the UK Government's Cabinet Office. Its ambitious mission was to influence areas of policy, spread understanding of behavioural approaches in central government administration, and achieve at least a tenfold return on the costs of the unit (Halpern, 2015, p. 54). The BIT rapidly became known as the 'nudge unit'. Although met with initial suspicion, the team soon demonstrated how behavioural science principles could be used to achieve good outcomes.

One challenge that it faced was that of reducing government spending on fighting fraud, error, and debt (Behavioural Insights Team, 2012) The team trialled interventions to increase the number of people paying by Direct Debit in fifteen London boroughs—this made council tax collection much more efficient. Tax payers were automatically entered into a £25,000 prize draw if they signed up to direct debit payments. For a £25,000 outlay, the boroughs received efficiency savings of £345,000. Each borough's investment was paid back in just three months.

The BIT developed frameworks that could be used across government departments. In 2010, the BIT published the MINDSPACE report and framework (Dolan, Hallsworth, Halpern, King, & Vlaev, 2010) to help policy makers design new interventions. In 2014, it released an article describing four simple ways to apply behavioural insights—the EAST framework (easy, attractive, simple, and timely) (Service et al., 2014) Although these frameworks drew on decades of academic research, they were written for people with no behavioural science background. The BIT emphasised the importance of experimentation for evaluating their policy ideas and produced evidence on what worked and what didn't. The BIT was very successful. It is now a social purpose company, partly owned by the UK government and partly by its employees, and it advises other countries on how to set up their own BITs.

The US Social and Behavioural Science Team, established by President Obama to improve federal policies and programmes, was disbanded when President Trump came into power. However, BITs have now been set up in many different countries, including New Zealand, Australia, Canada, France, Qatar, and Singapore.

We've now seen how, with a better understanding of people's cognitive biases, we can change the choice architecture to nudge people to behave in ways that give better outcomes. However, these successes are in very specific situations, and the principles are ineffective in others. 'Nudges' provide behavioural solutions to problems that arise because of problems in human decision making. There are many other factors that affect behaviour, and there is more to behaviour change than nudging.

1.1.3   From Social and Health Psychology: Modelling Human Behaviour

We've seen theories that developed following challenges to classical economics, and we understand how those have been applied in government. However, more evidence informing our views on human behaviour arose from social and health psychology, that viewed behaviour in a slightly different way.

Social psychology explores how people interact with each other and how a person's thoughts, feelings and behaviours are influenced by the real or imagined presence of other people (Allport, 1935). Health psychology focusses specifically on the psychological processes and cultural factors that influence our health and wellness behaviour. Both of these areas of psychology investigated human behaviour scientifically, developing testable hypotheses and constructing theories and models of behaviour.[3] Unlike the two earlier approaches, which focussed on limiting the impact of cognitive biases, social psychologists knew that the complexity of behavioural systems meant that a single intervention was unlikely to change behaviour.

Social psychology considers emotions, attitudes and beliefs, how people perceive themselves and their identity, how they make attributions about others, how they behave in groups, and why they behave altruistically or aggressively. Behavioural economists focus on the wide range of cognitive biases and defaults that influence judgments of value, but social psychologists try to understand the *processes* that people go through when making decisions. They have investigated the processes that affect how our beliefs are formed, how we change our attitudes, and how we can influence and persuade people to change their behaviour.

Some of these ideas have entered popular discourse. One of these is the idea of cognitive dissonance (Festinger, 1957). This is the tension that occurs when a person holds two seemingly opposing views at the same time. People prefer harmony in their beliefs and behaviours, and so they will generally change or reject one of the views to remove tension.

---

[3] Psychologists can be rather loose in their terminology and often use the words theory and model interchangeably. For our purposes, we use theory to mean a concept that explains when and why a behaviour occurs and model to mean a representation of how different factors interact and relate to each other to cause a behaviour. This is discussed in more detail in Chap. 3.

Health psychologists seek to promote healthy behaviours in the population, and they design interventions to encourage and support people in making better health decisions. In common with the social psychologists, they use theoretical models to understand which factors result in specific behaviours. These models help them identify those factors that need to be influenced in order for behaviour to change. An example of such a model used by social and health psychologists is the Theory of Planned Behaviour (Azjen, 1991). This theory has been widely adopted for designing health interventions and has also been applied in marketing and advertising. The basic idea is that your intention to do something is determined by your attitudes to the behaviour, by what you consider to be 'normal' in society and by whether or not you think you are able to perform the behaviour. And your intention to do something is the main influence on whether or not you actually do it.

The thinking of social and health psychologists really shaped the development of behavioural science. Theories like the Theory of Planned Behaviour (Ajzen, 1991) are useful because they provide a model of how people see the world, and can provide an explanation for why, when and how a behaviour does or does not occur. These theories are often imperfect simplifications, but they provide a reliable way to approach behavioural problems and to make predictions about human behaviour. Social and health psychologists use these theories to design interventions to change behaviour to enable people to lose weight or to stop smoking.

There are many behavioural theories, focussing on beliefs, rational behaviour, emotions, habits, and other areas. One book lists 83 behavioural theories (Michie, Campbell, Brown, West, & Gainforth, 2014). Few behavioural scientists will use all of these theories, and very few non-behavioural scientists will ever have heard of them.

Nevertheless, there are some models that are broadly applicable and are widely used. One of these is the COM-B (Michie, van Stralen, & West, 2011) model (Capability, Opportunity, Motivation—Behaviour). This was developed by Professor **Susan Michie** and her team at University College London. It conceptualises behaviour as a system of interacting elements that involve capability, opportunity and motivation. If you perform a behaviour at any given moment, you must be physically or psychologically capable of doing it, you must have the social or physical opportunity to do it, and you must be motivated to do it (either through conscious thought or through an automatic response). This theory enables us to explore the influences on any given behaviour in any situation—it's widely applicable and can be used as a behavioural diagnostic.

The social and health psychologists gave us theories and models that can be systematically tested and validated, and which enable us to consider behaviour and behaviour change from a greater number of perspectives. Finally, these frameworks definitively explain why we need to intervene at several different points to encourage effective behaviour change.

1.2 WHY DON'T BUSINESSES MAKE MORE USE OF BEHAVIOURAL SCIENCE?

We've seen how the discipline of behavioural science has been developed and applied both academically and in the public government sector. However, as of 2018, the private sector has been slow to embrace it. This seems rather surprising. Businesses make things or offer services that almost always involve people, and many of their products or services require people to change their behaviour. They might need people to do more of something (save money for the future), do less of something (use less energy), or do something different (buy a new product).

So why don't businesses do more behavioural science? Perhaps it's because of inertia. Businesses often have long-established ways for doing innovation and for bringing products and services to market. Businesses, much like individuals, don't readily change their behaviour. From our work with clients at Innovia, there seem to be five barriers to incorporating behavioural science into the business of business.

Barrier 1: 'That sounds like what we already do'. Many marketing departments already collect data, conduct research into what consumers want, and seek consumer insight. For them, the behavioural science approach can sound like 'old wine in new bottles.' But although behavioural science concepts seem familiar, there are also differences. A lot of marketing intelligence focuses on usage and attitudes rather than on actual behaviour. In contrast, behavioural science focuses only on those factors that drive or change behaviour directly or indirectly. Marketing departments seek to collect data to inform their decisions but rarely use an underlying model or theory to guide their thinking about what the data means. This means that the factors on which they base strategy may be at best peripheral, and at worst irrelevant, to the relevant behaviour. A further difference is that marketing departments rarely use a 'control' case when testing a new concept with the consumer, whereas a behavioural science approach will generally check whether an intervention works when compared with a control condition without it.

Barrier 2: 'This will take too long'. Businesses move at a much faster pace than academia or public policy. A behavioural science approach requires a rigorous, systematic analysis of the problem before identifying and prioritising suitable solutions. Existing approaches are quick and can seem 'good enough', and many commercial organisations either lack the knowledge base or are unwilling to invest the time or effort to apply behavioural science principles.

Barrier 3: 'It sounds good but where would we put behavioural scientists?' The structure of organisations can be an impediment to incorporating and integrating a new way of thinking. Where should a behavioural scientist live in an organisation? Should she be part of marketing? Or R&D? Or a separate department? Where would he add most value? There's no good answer—if an organisation creates an entirely new function, the function may be peripheral so will have little impact. If behavioural science is integrated into an existing function, it may be swamped by more tried-and-tested ways of doing things.

Barrier 4: 'We do R&D: thinking about the consumer is not the key focus for us'. When designing new products and services, there seem to be two schools of thought. The first is that 'we need to really understand what the consumer needs and wants.' The second is that 'consumers don't know what they want until you show it to them'. The truth generally lies somewhere in between. If we design something truly novel that consumers have no experience of, they may not know that they need it. On the other hand, without having some idea of what needs we are designing for, it is hard to know what to invent. Many R&D functions rely on their commercial partners to supply them with enough information about user needs in order to develop an innovation pipeline. However, we've already seen why some information from marketing teams may not be as reliable as hoped.

Barrier 5: 'We don't sell to consumers'. Business-to-business (B2B) companies may not see why behavioural science applies to them. They believe that their own customers make conscious, rational decisions based on explicit data. However, although their customers are businesses, businesses are still run by humans. Humans making decisions on behalf of companies behave in very similar ways to humans making decisions on behalf of themselves. Most of those decisions are unconscious and often irrational (Ariely, 2009). Additionally, B2B companies can still use behavioural science to promote good behaviour within the company, as well as from their customers.

Don't take these barriers lightly. In the rest of this book, we explore how to use behavioural science and how to overcome these five challenges.

1.3   WHY SHOULD BUSINESSES USE BEHAVIOURAL SCIENCE?

There are many business activities that can be improved by application of behavioural science—in early-stage innovation, developing radical communication strategies, rethinking customer experiences, or asking employees to work differently. Additionally, businesses collect enormous quantities of data about customers and employees, so they have a lot of information they could use to work out what is driving their behaviour. Unfortunately, they rarely use the data in this way.

We see three major reasons why the private sector should make better use of behavioural science.

1. *An evidence-based, experimental approach gives businesses a greater chance of success.* Using evidence-based science to understand human behaviour is more effective than relying on gut instinct or biases. The scientific method uses theory and evidence to ensure that we are focussing on the right problem, to develop testable hypotheses, and to design experiments to test them. As a result, we can design products, services, and interventions that have a greater chance of success.

2. *People don't always do what they say they do.* Using theory and models of behaviour helps us to understand why people do what they do, not what they say they do. People can't tell us exactly how they will behave, because they don't appreciate all the factors that influence their behaviours, especially those factors that are emotional, unconscious, or environmental. If businesses rely just on what people tell them, their products and services may fail.

3. *Behavioural models make data analysis more efficient.* When analysing data from observing consumers, there are many variables that might be associated with behaviours. It is often hard to narrow these down to a key set. Having a framework to explain what drives behaviour helps us to navigate complexity and focus on the right things, whilst ignoring those that are interesting but irrelevant.

Ultimately, behavioural science can be used to better understand human behaviour so that we can design services and products that meet people's needs, that are acceptable to them and that they will use.

REFERENCES

Agarwal, S., Chomsisengphet, S., Mahoney, N., & Stroebel, J. (2015). Regulating consumer financial products: Evidence from credit cards. *Quarterly Journal of Economics*, 1–54. https://doi.org/10.1093/qje/qju037

Ajzen, I. (1991). The theory of planned behavior. *Organizational Behavior and Human Decision Processes, 50*, 179–211.

Allport, G. W. (1935). Attitudes. In *Handbook of social psychology* (Vol. 1, pp. 789–844). Worcester, MA: Clark University Press.

Ariely, D. (2009). *Predictably irrational: The hidden forces that shape our decisions*. London: HarperCollins.

Behavioural Insights Team. (2012). *Applying behavioural insights to reduce fraud, error and debt*. Cabinet Office. Retrieved from https://assets.publishing.service.gov.uk/government/uploads/system/uploads/attachment_data/file/60539/BIT_FraudErrorDebt_accessible.pdf

Dolan, P., Hallsworth, M., Halpern, D., King, D., & Vlaev, I. (2010). *MINDSPACE: Influencing behaviour through public policy*. Cabinet Office; Institute for Government. Retrieved from http://38r8om2xjhhl25mw24492dir.wpengine.netdna-cdn.com/wp-content/uploads/2015/07/MINDSPACE.pdf

Festinger, L. (1957). *A theory of cognitive dissonance*. Evanston, IL: Row & Peterson.

Halpern, D. (2015). *Inside the Nudge Unit: How small changes can make a big difference*. London: WH Allen.

Kahneman, D. (2012). *Thinking, fast and slow*. London: Penguin.

Kahneman, D., & Tversky, A. (1979). Prospect Theory: An analysis of decision under risk. *Econometrica, 47*(2), 263–292.

List of cognitive biases. (2016). In *Wikipedia, the free encyclopedia*. Retrieved from https://en.wikipedia.org/w/index.php?title=List_of_cognitive_biases&oldid=725970762

Lunn, P. (2014). *Regulatory policy and behavioural economics*. Paris: Organisation for Economic Co-operation and Development. Retrieved from http://www.oecd-ilibrary.org/content/book/9789264207851-en

Michie, S., Campbell, R., Brown, R., West, R., & Gainforth, H. (2014). *The ABC of behaviour change theories* (1st ed.). London: Silverback Publishing.

Michie, S., van Stralen, M. M., & West, R. (2011). The behaviour change wheel: A new method for characterising and designing behaviour change interventions. *Implementation Science, 6*, –42. https://doi.org/10.1186/1748-5908-6-42

Service, O., Hallsworth, H., Halpern, D., Algate, F., Gallagher, R., Nguyen, S., ... Sanders, M. (2014). *EAST: Four simple ways to apply behavioural insights*. Cabinet Office. Retrieved from https://www.behaviouralinsights.co.uk/publications/east-four-simple-ways-to-apply-behavioural-insights/

Simon, H. A. (1947). *Administrative behavior: A study of decision-making processes in administrative organizations*. New York, NY: Macmillan.

Sunstein, C. R. (2012). *The office of information and regulatory affairs: Myths and realities* (SSRN Scholarly Paper No. ID 2192639). Rochester, NY: Social Science Research Network. Retrieved from http://papers.ssrn.com/abstract=2192639

Sunstein, C. R., & Thaler, R. H. (2009). *Nudge: Improving decisions about health, wealth and happiness*. London: Penguin.

Tversky, A., & Kahneman, D. (1974). Judgment under uncertainty: Heuristics and biases. *Science, 185*(4157), 1124–1131. https://doi.org/10.1126/science.185.4157.1124

West, R. (2015). The P.R.I.M.E. theory of motivation as a possible foundation for the treatment of addiction. In *Addiction treatment: Science and policy for the twenty-first century*. Baltimore, MD: John Hopkins University Press.

CHAPTER 2

The Difficulty of Predicting Behaviour

Why Existing Market Research Methods Aren't Good Enough

Abstract Businesses want to change behaviour but conventional market research processes are often poor at predicting it. Predicting behaviour is hard and the intention–behaviour gap is significant. Conventional market research methods make it even harder because the data is often poor quality, data is confused with insight, data collection fails to focus on the factors that drive behaviour and a lot of research is done to confirm existing biases rather than to prove or refute behavioural hypotheses. Rubinstein discusses the barriers to gaining a deeper understanding of consumer behaviour and makes the case for better research tools and methods that apply the principles of behavioural science. In particular, she discusses the importance of having a good theoretical framework to allow researchers to find out what people really do, not what they say they do.

Keywords Consumer behaviour • Consumer insight • Intention–behaviour gap • Market research methods

Katie, a health psychologist, and I were just starting out on a new project to encourage people to take their prescription drugs correctly—to increase their 'compliance to medication'. We were surrounded by dozens of research reports that our client had sent us, and we were feeling frustrated. We'd ploughed through acres of

© The Author(s) 2018
H. Rubinstein, *Applying Behavioural Science to the Private Sector*,
https://doi.org/10.1007/978-3-030-01698-2_2

technical reports, usage and attitude studies, focus groups and surveys, only to find that most of the information failed to get to the
nub of the problem. What was it all for? Which parts were important
and which irrelevant? Why was it repetitive and lacking focus? How
could there be so much data, yet so little insight?

"I can't seem to find anything useful in this about compliance!" Katie
dumped yet another sheaf of papers onto the desk.

"I guess the data must have been collected for some other reason," I
responded.

*"I think I've read the same report three times, just with different
dates on,"* she laughed. *"And I still don't know what factors influence
poor compliance. There are lots of quotes but no hypotheses, and a lot of
the conclusions go way beyond the data I can see here! It must have cost
a fortune to do this research, but I doubt the company got very much out
of it at all."*

"Get used to it," I said. *"Lots of companies commission the same
research every year. They do exactly what they have done before because
that is the way they have always done it. This means that they miss out
on critical factors that might be important."*

Katie looked surprised. *"But surely it matters that we understand
why people aren't taking their medication correctly? If we don't know
that, we can't prioritise potential approaches because we don't know
which are more likely to work. From these pieces of research, I can't tell
which factors are more important than others at affecting how people
take their medication?"*

*   *   *

As this discussion illustrates, conventional market research processes are
often poor at predicting human behaviour. This chapter discusses how we
can do better.

Businesses want to change behaviour. They often want people to do
more of something (such as buy a product more often), or *less* of something (such as use smaller amounts of a concentrated washing up liquid)
or do something *differently* (such as try a new technology). A great deal of
research aims to find out how people respond if they are asked to buy
more, do less or behave differently. Researchers often ask survey questions

such as, *'How likely are you to buy this product in the next three months?'* or *'If this facility was near you, would you recycle your goods?'* They then assume that these measures of intent indicate how successful the new product or approach will be in the market.

But they are sadly mistaken. Human behaviour is complicated and predicting it is hard. What these researchers don't realise is that there is a gap between intention and actual behaviour. This means that their approaches often fall short of accurately predicting what people will do. And that can mean the difference between a product's success or failure.

2.1   WHY DOES THE INTENTION–BEHAVIOUR GAP MAKE PREDICTING BEHAVIOUR HARD?

If a person decides to do something (intention), then they are more likely to actually do it (behaviour) (Sheeran, 2002). However, any number of things can intervene between the intention and the behaviour (Box 2.1). Sometimes, you can be really motivated to do something and yet still not do it! Intentions and beliefs about what is good or bad only influence our actions if they create sufficiently strong wants and needs at the relevant moment (West, 2015). You can get distracted at the last minute and not do what you said or thought you would. Or, regardless of what you intended, you actually just try to get what you want most at that specific moment without really thinking about it.

It's clear that people do not always do what they said they'll do: not because they are being mischievous or lying, but because they just don't notice this disconnect between their behaviour and their intentions.

In order to get better at predicting behaviour, we need to understand peoples' wants and needs in the relevant context, including how they think about themselves (their self-image) and the behavioural patterns that they've established, based on what they have done in the past. And the research that we conduct needs to get better at identifying those factors that really influence behaviour and avoid getting distracted by those that don't.

Box 2.1 The Intention–Behaviour Gap Makes Prediction Hard
Predicting behaviour is hard, not least because there are so many possible factors that might influence us. Imagine that you intend to

get fit. A local gym is offering a great deal on annual membership. Their leaflet says that spending only $10 a month is the best way to good health. The gym is only five minutes away from where you live, and its monthly fees seem affordable. The first consideration is whether you believe that doing more exercise will improve your health, and whether going to a gym is the best way to achieve this. Another consideration is whether you believe that people whose opinion you respect would approve of your decision to buy a gym membership. If your best friend thinks it is a waste of money, you may decide not to bother. Even if you think joining a gym is a good way to improve your health and your best friend agrees, you may worry that you may not be capable of using the membership often enough to get the full benefit. These are just three of the typical influences that determine whether or not we intend to do something.

From a psychological perspective, your self-image is also important in determining whether or not you will take out a membership. You may have read that doing more exercise will improve your health. You may even think that you have time to go to a gym once a week to achieve this. But you might not join the gym because you just don't see yourself as the sort of person who goes to a gym. Maybe you don't think you have much in common with the people you know who go to gyms. Perhaps you think of yourself as someone who prefers to walk or go out dancing instead.

And an obvious (but often overlooked) reason for doing something is that you have done it before—behaviour can influence attitudes as much as attitudes can influence behaviour. If you used to have a gym membership but it has lapsed, you might be more willing to get another one. But if you have never had one before, you may think that you don't need one now—past behaviour may be the best predictor of future behaviour.

All these factors may influence your intentions and ultimately your behaviour. We need to consider these when conducting research.

2.2   Why Do We Need Better Research Tools and Methods?

Most companies spend a lot of time, effort, and money working out what motivates people, how to meet their needs, and how to get people to engage with their products and services. But this money is often not well spent.

Knowing what to do in order to get people to engage with your product and service is particularly critical when designing something that is innovative—something that people have not seen before. Innovation is a risky business. The popular statistic is that between 80% and 90% of new products introduced in the market fail. This figure differs depending on the industry and when and how success is measured, but it certainly shows that we need a better way of predicting what products people will actually buy in the market.

Using behavioural science can give companies confidence in their product development and innovation. This is because behavioural science focuses on identifying the factors, benefits and attributes that really *drive behaviour and decisions* in the real world.

It's clear that businesses need a new approach. Many senior managers complain that despite all the investment their company has made in understanding people, many of their products and services still fail. There might be many reasons for failure—poor product quality, inadequate distribution or getting the timing of the launch wrong. However, managers often say that products fail because the business hasn't identified exactly what people want (Castellion & Markham, 2013; Crawford, 1977). Examples of reasons for failure include:

- not identifying problems early enough because of poor research
- targeting the wrong market
- incorrectly predicting what people would pay for the product or service
- finding that consumers didn't want the product or service once launched

How can products fail like this, when so much market research has been conducted, prototypes have been tested with users, communications have been developed and usage trials have been completed? Even more surprisingly, research suggests that products fail even if the consumers liked the product and their intentions-to-purchase scores were high.

Do people do what they say they'll do? No. It seems that people say one thing during the consumer research and do another in practice. Perhaps we need to change the research methods.

2.3   WHAT ARE THE PROBLEMS WITH TRADITIONAL RESEARCH TOOLS?

Typically, companies commission many expensive consumer and category research reports, which contain enormous amounts of data. These data are collected at great cost. Many companies are literally drowning in data!

Conventional market research often yields information that is not useful. This is for four reasons:

1. data generated is of poor quality: sloppy or naïve data generation and collection
2. data provides little insight: little or no interpretation or underlying model of behaviour
3. research does not recognise or focus on the factors that drive behaviour
4. research is commissioned, in effect, to confirm existing biases

The result of these four failures is that research rarely focuses on, or is informed by, the thing that really matters—consumer *behaviour.*

2.3.1   Data Generated Is of Poor Quality

Market research is multi-billion-dollar business,[1] and many companies are involved in collecting, analysing, and reporting on consumer data. Much of this data is collected automatically—via the surveys, ratings, and feedback forms received when products and services are purchased. This amount of data is historically unprecedented and should provide rich sources of information to guide business decisions. Businesses are drowning in data.

But abundant data is not necessarily useful data. The market research industry has known for years that certain types of people, usually with

---

[1] In 2016, the global market research industry was estimated to be valued at $44bn (https://www.statista.com/statistics/242477/global-revenue-of-market-research-companies/).

negative or extreme opinions, are more likely to complete surveys. This means that results from surveys can be biased because they do not represent the views of the majority of the population.

Even if market research is targeted at the right people, they don't always seem to tell 'the truth'. They don't consciously lie to researchers, but they are likely to succumb to what psychologists refer to as 'desirability bias'— the tendency for respondents to answer questions in a way that will be viewed favourably by the interviewer and others around them. This bias may be exaggerated because most people are paid to participate in market research and so feel subconsciously obliged to respond in the way they think the researcher wants.

And we should not underestimate the power of peer-group pressure. In a social situation, such as a focus group, people will tend to be influenced by the responses of others, resulting in a sort of 'groupthink' (Janis, 1982) that follows the most vociferous.

Added to these issues, companies are finding it more difficult to get good access to quality data because of privacy and security concerns. Consumers are increasingly aware that companies collect data about them and some will withhold information from companies they do not trust (The Psychometrics Centre, Innovia Technology, & Edelman, 2016).

In summary, data can be unrepresentative, inaccurate, and biased. To get good data, you need to understand how psychology and behaviour can influence your data source.

2.3.2   Data Provides Little Insight

The very words 'consumer insight' strike fear into the hearts of innovation practitioners because real insight is rare. Insight is the holy grail of research. Researchers seek the 'truth' about the user, based on their beliefs, behaviours, and experiences. Or better still, they want to peer into the future to spot a trend that no one else has yet seen. Companies hope that, armed with a unique insight, they can create a differentiated product or service that consumers want.

But what does the word 'insight' actually mean? Sometimes, it is used to describe raw data, or a factoid—an unreliable piece of information that seems to be interesting but does not really have much influence on what is going on. Sometimes, it is used to describe a statement of need. However, unless you know which needs are more critical than others, or whether there are some needs that exist that are not being met, statements of need are no more insightful than random facts. A true insight is based not only on an understanding what motivates consumers, but on knowledge of what factors are driving their behaviour.

Insights are rare and hard to find. Finding them requires experience, structure, and careful thought. The structure can be provided by a behavioural model or theoretical framework. The behavioural model or theoretical framework (discussed in Chap. 3) is itself based on valuable insights about the market or users. Companies can spend a lot of time, effort, and money on looking for insights, but they are unlikely to find them if they are looking in the wrong place, don't have a suitable structure or framework, or suffer from the three other common research problems described here.

In summary, good insights are best found by processing data through a meaningful, proven, and structured framework.

2.3.3   Research Doesn't Focus on the Factors That Drive Behaviour

We've seen why survey-based data often doesn't tell us how people choose things in the real world. Survey methodologies succumb to the problem of the 'cognitive response paradigm', described by the psychologist, Richard Bagozzi (2006). He said that there were several issues with consumer-based research including a lack of understanding of the different factors that determine behaviour or of the relative importance of these factors. Furthermore, a lot of consumer research focuses primarily on how a decision is made but ignores what happens when decisions are monitored, changed or abandoned. And finally, a lot of consumer research relies purely on rationality as the basis for the decision.

This type of research tacitly assumes that we make deliberative decisions where we have carefully thought through the options, weighed up the benefits and disadvantages, and made a rational decision. The way surveys are written follows from this: they consist of a sequential string of questions asking people for their most important product attribute, how much they would be prepared to pay, and how the product compares with others on the market. The people being surveyed try hard to answer these questions as well and thoughtfully as they can, but this does not remotely resemble the actual process they go through when they are standing in the store or clicking the "buy" button online.

In reality, there are lots of reasons why people do or do not buy a product and many of them are social, emotional and unconscious. People may:

- avoid a product because it simply does not fit with their image of themselves (something psychologists call self-identity)
- buy a product on impulse because they are in a good mood, with no deep thinking involved at all
- buy a product because they bought it before and it has become a habit
- choose a product because people they know are buying it, so they feel they should too
- avoid a product because they associate it with a taboo, either consciously or unconsciously

Conventional surveys often don't consider these motivations, and neither do consumers when rationally answering the survey questions.

In summary, good research considers the subtle array of emotional, social, and cultural drivers of behaviour that determine what people do in the real world.

2.3.4   *Research Is Commissioned to Confirm Existing Biases*

Most clients who commission surveys do so with an ingoing hypothesis or bias about what they want to find. This is understandable—they often want to confirm the value of the work they have been doing already. It takes a great deal of discipline and courage not to embed those biases into the survey method or content. The biases are often not immediately apparent—it could merely be that there are more questions about the favoured option, or that there are no alternative questions that could validate a contradictory hypothesis. Consumer research too seldom tries to disprove an ingoing hypothesis or asks questions of the consumers in a truly open-ended way.

Also, many surveys are commissioned to provide an update on previous information. This may be useful to measure small changes, such as whether people are buying more or less than before. However, this entrenches beliefs about what it is important to measure, further embedding the hypotheses or beliefs on which the original data collection was based. It very rarely sets out open-mindedly to check or refute them.

In summary, good research will approach the consumer with an open mind and open method. It will be designed with the intent of refuting, as well as proving, prior hypotheses.

2.4   Why Does Behavioural Science Enable Better Research and Better Understanding?

From the analysis above, we can conclude that:

- good data collection should be supported by a clear understanding of how psychology and behaviour can influence the data source
- good insights are best found by processing data through a meaningful, proven behavioural model or theoretical framework
- good research must consider the subtle array of emotional, social, and cultural drivers of behaviour that determine what people do in the real world
- good research will approach the consumer with an open mind and open method, and with the intent of refuting as well as proving prior hypotheses

Behavioural science theory and models can help to address these goals. Over the past few decades, researchers in the field have investigated what drives behaviour. They have developed and tested theories and models that focus on the factors that influence behaviour change, and on the real processes that people go through when they make judgments and decisions. There are examples of models and theories in Chaps. 3 and 4.

No model is perfect because all models are simplifications of the complex real world. Nevertheless, models are useful because they offer a coherent description of why, when, and how a behaviour does or does not occur. The components of the models have been tested and validated in a variety of contexts and have been found to be usefully predictive.

Using an appropriate behavioural science model can help to avoid the problems of collecting poor-quality or irrelevant data, because it helps us to focus on factors that really matter and ignore those that don't. Behavioural science recognises that decision-making is driven as much by habitual, emotional, socially conditioned, or automatic responses as it is by considered, rational, or thoughtful ones. If we include these responses in our analysis, we are better able to understand why people don't always do exactly what they say they'll do, and we will find out how to better predict their behaviour.

When we choose the right behavioural model, we can make sense of the data and its relevance to the behaviours we want to influence. This leads us to valuable insights and well-targeted interventions that influence behaviour.

Finally, if we approach the research design with an open mindset and use the scientific method, we can more easily notice and eliminate ingoing bias, and recognise that there is valuable information for us whether or not our hypotheses are supported by the results.

2.5   SUMMARY

Behavioural science has the potential to improve the way we do research with consumers and to ensure that the results we get tell us more about what people actually do, not just what they say they'll do.

Innovation is a risky business and the failure rate is high. Traditional approaches to consumer research have many shortcomings and may exacerbate the problem. A major contributing factor is that data collection focuses on what people say they do rather than on what is actually driving behaviour.

There are four critical problems that can undermine the relevance of research aimed at understanding whether consumers will engage with a new product or service.

Bad research:

1. Generates poor-quality data, because the research is not supported by a clear understanding of how psychology and behaviour can influence the data source
2. Confuses data with insight, because data processing is not done through a meaningful, proven behavioural model or structured theoretical framework
3. Fails to recognise the factors that drive behaviour, because the data collection does not capture the subtle array of social, emotional, and cultural drivers of behaviour that determine what people do in the real world
4. Confirms existing biases, because the research is not approached with an open mind or open methods and is not intent on refuting, as well as proving, prior hypotheses

The intention–behaviour gap is substantial. Nevertheless, a behavioural science approach can begin to narrow the gap. Using an appropriate model or theory of behaviour helps to avoid the problems of collecting poorly focussed data, and ensures that the habitual, emotional, socially conditioned, or automatic responses are included in the subsequent analysis. A theoretical underpinning helps to target the areas that can be influenced and to avoid focussing on those areas that will be of minimal relevance. If we approach research design with an open mindset and use the scientific method, we can eliminate biases and get more meaningful results. Behavioural science has the potential to improve the way we do research with consumers to ensure that we know more about what people actually do, not just what they say they'll do.

References

Bagozzi, R. P. (2006). Explaining consumer behaviour and consumer action: From fragmentation to unity. *Seoul Journal of Business, 12*(2), 11–143.

Castellion, G., & Markham, S. K. (2013). Perspective: New product failure rates: Influence of argumentum ad populum and self-interest. *Journal of Product Innovation Management, 30*(5), 976–979. https://doi.org/10.1111/j.1540-5885.2012.01009.x

Crawford, C. M. (1977). Marketing research and the new product failure rate. *Journal of Marketing, 41*(2), 51–61.

Janis, I. L. (1982). *Groupthink: Psychological studies of policy decisions and fiascoes* (6th ed.). Boston: Houghton Mifflin.

Sheeran, P. (2002). Intention–behavior relations: A conceptual and empirical review. *European Review of Social Psychology, 12*(1), 1–36. https://doi.org/10.1080/14792772143000003

The Psychometrics Centre, Innovia Technology, & Edelman. (2016). *Trust and Predictive Technologies 2016 Report*. London.

West, R. (2015). The P.R.I.M.E. theory of motivation as a possible foundation for the treatment of addiction. In *Addiction treatment: Science and policy for the twenty-first century*. Baltimore, MD: John Hopkins Univeristy Press.

CHAPTER 3

The Science Behind Behaviour

Why Evidence-Based Theories and Models Are Useful

Abstract This chapter describes how theories and models of behaviour provide focus, help to cut through complexity and guide decisions about what products, services and interventions to design and develop. Rubinstein argues that too many businesses focus on changing attitudes and beliefs rather than on the behaviours themselves and that without a good theory or model of behaviour, companies do not know what activities to observe, or what is really important in influencing behaviour. She defines what makes a good theory or model of behaviour and how to use and develop models to understand specific challenges. She uses the COM-B and the Unified Theory of Acceptance and Use of Technology to illustrate how theories benefit decision-making and how they can be used in practice.

Keywords Acceptance and Use of Technology Model • Attitudes • Behavioural theory • COM-B

Before we look at how to apply behavioural science, let's define exactly what we mean by behaviour, and let's explore the sort of theories and models that we use to explain it.

© The Author(s) 2018
H. Rubinstein, *Applying Behavioural Science to the Private Sector*,
https://doi.org/10.1007/978-3-030-01698-2_3

3.1   What Is Behaviour? What Causes It?

We define behaviour as anything a person does in response to internal or external events. A behaviour can be overt and observable, like performing a physical action or telling someone to do something. It can also be covert or not observable, like reading silently or thinking about a problem. Unobservable behaviours are typically mental processes. Many unobservable behaviours still result in observable actions.

It's sometimes hard to differentiate between a behaviour, things that affect a behaviour (determinants), and things that are affected by a behaviour (outcomes). Riding a bicycle is a behaviour but having the confidence to ride the bicycle is a determinant of that behaviour. Dieting is a behaviour but losing weight is an outcome. Intending to eat two small meals a day is a determinant of the behaviour of dieting. It may or may not result in the desired outcome of losing weight.

When people confuse behaviours, determinants, and outcomes, they may focus on the wrong aspect, and so the interventions won't work. Businesses often fail to specify the desired behaviour in sufficient detail, or they target a single specific determinant of a behaviour without knowing how important it is or how it interacts with other determinants of the behaviour. It's really important that the difference between these elements is understood.

Businesses often try to change attitudes. An attitude is a determinant of a behaviour, not a behaviour. Psychologists define an attitude as the enduring organisation of beliefs, feelings and behavioural tendencies towards others, events and objects (Hogg & Vaughn, 2005, p. 150). People often mistakenly think that if they change an attitude or belief, then they will necessarily change connected behaviour. Organisations spend a great deal of effort, time and money trying to change people's attitudes—however people's behaviour is affected by much more than just their attitude.

Let's imagine a perfume manufacturer who wants to convince its consumers that its perfumes are for sophisticated and elegant women. It spends a lot of money redesigning the packaging and communications. Women notice the changes and tell researchers that the new perfume looks sophisticated and elegant. But the manufacturer is frustrated—there is no change in sales! Even though it has successfully changed attitudes, women are still not buying the perfume. Something else is affecting their behaviour. Perhaps the women don't have enough money to purchase it. Perhaps the sophisticated and elegant image doesn't fit with their self-identity. Changing attitudes alone is rarely enough to change behaviour.

The evidence shows that attitudes actually have a very limited influence on behaviour (Glasman & Albarracín, 2006). There may be a correlation (relationship) between an attitude and a behaviour but this doesn't mean that having a particular attitude causes a behaviour. Attitudes do affect behaviour, but only under certain conditions. Other determinants are important too.

In most situations, we want to change behaviour, not just influence attitudes, beliefs, or other determinants. Most businesses want to change behaviour because they want to increase sales. But behaviour is complex and there are multiple factors that can influence it. We need to know how to work out which factors matter, and which do not. We need a way to organise and prioritise these factors.

3.2   What Is a Theory? What Is a Model? And How Do They Help Our Understanding?

Imagine that you are worried about a symptom you have, and you want to get it investigated. You have a theory that the best way of getting this symptom investigated is to go and consult your local doctor. Your friend agrees with this theory. You have a mental model of what you expect from the consultation. You expect the doctor to give you direct, simple advice and a prescription for a medication. Your friend, however, has a completely different mental model of what they would expect from the consultation. They would expect to be informed of all of their different options and to actively choose which treatment option would work best for them.

Theories can form the basis of models, but sometimes there might be several models of one theory. A theory is a system of ideas, and a model is a representation of what that system actually looks like. In behavioural science, we use these terms frequently. We say that theories are systems of ideas or factors that explain a behaviour and models actually define how these factors affect each other. A theory is a generalised overview, and a model is a purposeful representation of reality. Theories and models help us to explore the causes of a behaviour that we want to influence.

So, behavioural theories explain why, when and how a behaviour does or does not occur, and they show the important sources of influence that can alter the behaviour. They help us to generate testable hypotheses and to make predictions about what might happen in the future. As the father of social psychology, Kurt Lewin, is quoted as saying "there is nothing as practical as a good theory" (Hogg & Vaughn, 2005, p. 35).

Models have three purposes: they are used to understand something that already exists (such as trying to understand how people make sense of current health and safety rules), to make something exist (such as trying to work out how people might engage with autonomous vehicles that are not yet on the roads) or to provoke new thinking (such as trying to work out to how get more people to be vaccinated). Models are always simplifications of the real world and although they can sometimes oversimplify, they are useful to us because they enable us to make sense of what is happening and define the relationship between cause and effect.

The models that have been developed to explain behaviours recognise that behaviour is a complex and dynamic system that is influenced by multiple factors. They demonstrate that there is unlikely to be one simple solution to change behaviour: many things influence our intentions, and our motivations can change from minute to minute.

3.3   WHY ARE THERE SO MANY THEORIES OF BEHAVIOUR?

There are many theories to explain behaviour and there is no one universal theory. Behaviour is situation and context-dependent and so an explanation for a behaviour in one situation may not be applicable in another. Behaviour can be modelled in many different ways. There are dozens of theories and models of behaviour which address different aspects of behaviour and consider behaviour change in different ways (Darnton, 2008).

Each model is based on a different set of simplifying assumptions that apply to the complex reality in question. Different behavioural models seek to explain different aspects of behaviour (Holley, 2012). Some are diagnostic (Michie, Atkins, & West, 2014a), some focus on routine or habitual behaviour (Duhigg, 2013) while others focus on planned behaviour (Ajzen, 1991). Some represent changes to behaviour as people progress through a series of stages (DiClemente & Prochaska, 1982), some focus on people learning specific knowledge or skills (Fisher, Fisher, Williams, & Malloy, 1994), whilst others focus on societal influences to change behaviour (Rogers, 1962). To select a model for a specific behaviour, you need to know about the many different approaches to understanding behaviour. Experts in this field have significant experience of applying many different approaches in many different situations.

Sometimes it is necessary to develop a theory or model from scratch, but often there are pre-existing theories. These have already been used to assess behaviour in a wide range of situations and can be applied or adapted to your situation.

Theories are tested, validated, and sometimes challenged. An example of a challenged theory is the Theory of Planned Behaviour (TBP) (Ajzen, 1991), which is commonly used in health promotion and marketing. This simple model assumes that the best predictor of behaviour is the intention to perform that behaviour. Intentions are influenced by three factors: the attitude towards the behaviour, the subjective norms that surround the behaviour, and the amount of perceived behavioural control. It has attracted a great deal of criticism because, on average, it appears that it is capable of predicting only about 34% of the variance in behaviour (Godin & Kok, 1996). There have been calls for it to be retired (Sniehotta, Presseau, & Araújo-Soares, 2014) and several researchers have modified it to improve its utility (Conner, 2015; Connor & Armitage, 1998). Nevertheless, it has been found to be useful in some circumstances (Truong, 2009) and it has been argued that much of the problem is that it has been applied indiscriminately; a case of 'poor use of the theory rather than the theory being poor' (St Quinton, 2016).

Let's look at two examples of well-validated models to see how they can guide our thinking: the COM-B (Michie, van Stralen, & West, 2011) and the Unified Acceptance and Use of Technology Model (Venkatesh & Davis, 2000).

As discussed in Chap. 1, the COM-B model describes behaviour as a system of three main interacting contributory elements: for a behaviour to occur at any given moment a person must have the capability, the opportunity, and the motivation to perform it. The model can be applied to many situations and is particularly useful when embarking on a behaviour change programme for the first time—it helps to systematically identify the barriers to and promoters of a behaviour. There are subtypes of each of the main elements (see Box 3.1), and in fact those subtypes can be further split out for more detailed analysis.

In this model, the individual components can interact and create feedback and reinforcement. So, motivation can be influenced by both opportunity and capability, and feedback from behaviour can influence motivations, opportunity, or capability. For example, imagine that you are learning to play the piano. Your opportunity to play the piano increases if

Box 3.1 Diagnosing What Needs to Be Done to Change Behaviour

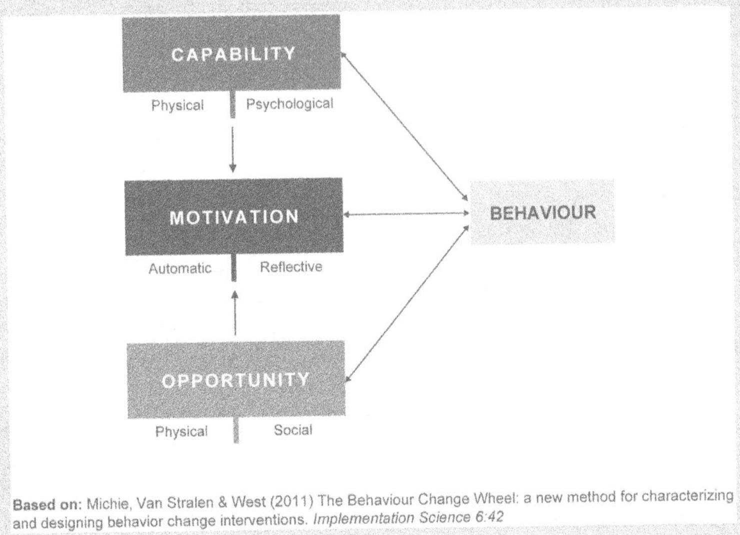
CAPABILITY
Physical
Psychological
MOTIVATION
Automatic
Reflective
OPPORTUNITY
Physical
Social
BEHAVIOUR
Based on: Michie, Van Stralen & West (2011) The Behaviour Change Wheel: a new method for characterizing and designing behavior change interventions. Implementation Science 6:42

Fig. 3.1 COM-B: making a behavioural diagnosis

C = capability. Capability can be both the psychological or physical capacity to perform a behaviour. ***Physical capability*** includes skill, strength, and stamina. This could be the ability to do something with practice, such as drive a car or develop good interpersonal skills through experience. ***Psychological capability*** includes the knowledge to perform a behaviour and the capacity to engage in the necessary thought processes. This could be through having knowledge of a topic or task, having a good enough memory to recall how to do something, or being able to pay attention to doing something. If someone lacks psychological capability, they may be cognitively overloaded, and too tired to perform a behaviour.

O = opportunity. Opportunity can be physical or social and refers to factors external to the person that can prompt or inhibit a behaviour. ***Physical opportunities*** can be created by the physical environment (such as time, financial resources, and access) whereas ***social opportunities*** are created by the cultural environment. Social

opportunities can be especially important as they relate to how people do things because of social norms, how they make social com-
parisons, and whether they identify with social groups.

M = motivation. Motivation refers to the processes in the brain
that energise and direct behaviour and includes unconscious processes (automatic motivations) and conscious decision-making
(reflective motivations). *Automatic* motivations can be emotions,
impulses, and habits whereas *reflective motivations* include evalua-
tions, plans, and beliefs—about one's own capabilities or about the
consequences of doing something.

your parents buy a piano for you to practice on. As you practice each day,
your motivation to play increases because you see an improvement. And as
your capability increases, you practice more and more.

Applying the COM-B model to existing data can yield new insights.
This reprocessing of old data has advantages: it does not replicate work
already completed, it may help to identify knowledge gaps, and it can help
to sort out large amounts of information in a structured way.

The COM-B model reminds us that there are many factors that contribute to a behaviour, and that if we identify the barriers and promoters,
we can design interventions that will change that behaviour.

The Unified Theory of Acceptance and Use of Technology (UTAUT)
(Venkatesh, Morris, Davis, & Davis, 2003) (Box 3.2) aims to explain a
person's intentions to use a tool—in this case, a technology—and how
they subsequently behave. It was originally developed to explain how people take up new computer technology. As with many theories of behaviour
change, it has its roots in the Theory of Reasoned Action (Fishbein, 1979),
which states that behaviour is primarily determined by the intention to
perform the behaviour, which in turn is determined by subjective norms
and attitudes to the behaviour.

The UTAUT has gone through several iterations but the central idea is
that acceptance and usage of technology is influenced by two fundamental
factors—*perceived usefulness* of the tool (described as performance expectancy—the beliefs about whether or not the technology will improve your
performance in a task) and *perceived ease of use* (described as effort expectancy—the beliefs a person holds about the amount of effort required to
use it).

Box 3.2 A Model of Technology Acceptance

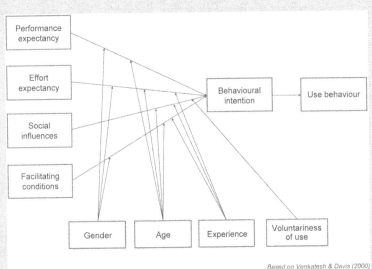

Based on Venkatesh & Davis (2000)

Fig. 3.2   The Unified Theory of Acceptance and Use of Technology

There are four key constructs in this model: performance expectancy, effort expectancy, social influences, and facilitating conditions. The first three directly influence the intention to use the technology (so only influence behaviour indirectly via intention) and the fourth directly influences user behaviour. Gender, age, experience, and voluntariness of use are moderating influences, and these determine how the four key constructs affect someone's usage intention and behaviour.

Performance expectancy is the strongest predictor of intention to use the technology and is defined as the degree to which a person believes that using the system will help him to improve performance.

Effort expectancy is defined as the degree of ease associated with the use of the system—how easy the person thinks it will be to use the system. Effort expectancy influences women more than men, especially older women who haven't often used the system.

Social influence is defined as the degree to which a person thinks that 'important others' believe she should use the new system. This works through three mechanisms: compliance, internalisation, and identification.

Belief in facilitating conditions is defined as the degree to which an individual believes that an organisational and technical infrastructure exists to support use of the system. Without this, the person cannot use the technology at all.

The model has been extended to include other important factors such as social influence and facilitating infrastructure. It has been good at predicting intentions and behaviour in real-life situations. It has been used to understand how people take up various different types of technology including whether doctors will accept a new telemedicine technology (Gagnon, Orruño, Asua, Abdeljelil, & Emparanza, 2012), how IT systems are used in universities (Jan & Contreras, 2011) and how people use cloud computing (Eltayeb & Dawson, 2016). In the longitudinal study to validate the theory, the UTAUT accounted for an impressive 70% of the variance in intention to use and about 50% in actual use.

3.4   How Do You Develop a Theory Relating to a Specific Behaviour?

Before embarking on a programme to change a behaviour, you need to have a theory about what is causing it, so you can test to see if your hypotheses are correct. If your hypotheses are incorrect, you may have to revise your assumptions before designing a product, service, or intervention. If your hypotheses prove to be correct, the product, service, or intervention that you design is more likely to be effective.

There are three steps to developing a sound theory to explain a specific behaviour:

1. Forming and testing hypotheses
2. Forming a coherent theory or model
3. Validating the model and making predictions

3.4.1   Form and Test Hypotheses

First, we need to develop hypotheses about what is causing the behaviour. Let's return to the example of solar road studs we discussed in Chap. 1. One initial hypothesis might be that some drivers, especially those that are novices, do not feel that they know what to do in certain situations on the highway. In psychology, this is a concept known as 'low self-efficacy': people believe that they don't have the capability to perform the behaviour to produce the desired outcome.

We cannot directly observe self-efficacy. So, to measure it, we have to find the right questions to ask of people and listen to what they say. In psychology, the list of right questions is called a construct[1]—a set of questions that, when combined, allow us to measure an unobservable behaviour.

We need to think carefully about the questions we use to represent self-efficacy and ensure that the ones we ask really are measuring this unobservable behaviour. Example indicators of self-efficacy might be 'not knowing the meaning of the signs on the highway', 'not knowing what the braking distances are when driving at high speeds,' and 'not having driven often enough on highways to feel confident'. Working out what are the right questions may seem complex and time consuming. However, like any good science experiment, particularly involving the unobservable, we need to understand what we are actually measuring so our deductions are sensible.

Of course, we must also consider other factors might influence driving behaviour. For example, a driver may be influenced by:

- How good a driver they think they are
- How worried they are about being penalised for bad driving
- How important they think it is to obey safety signals
- Whether they think tailgating is dangerous
- How likely drivers are to copy other people's behaviour when they are not sure what to do

3.4.2   Develop a Coherent Theory or Model

Once we have created our hypotheses about what determinants or other factors influence driving behaviour, and where possible, have checked them, we then need to understand how they relate to each other. For example, does one lead to another or are they independent and acting in parallel? To do this, we draw up a model that shows how they might all affect driving behaviour.

---

[1] There is a science to designing and testing constructs that are valid and reliable. If you want to know more, a good starter is Modern Psychometrics: The Science of Psychological Assessment by Rust and Golombok (2009) Routledge.

Getting the right model is not easy. It can be tempting to instinctively decide priority, or to assign causality, but we need to use our expertise and the scientific method. There are a number of well-tested and validated behavioural models, each of which represents specific types of influences on behaviours in different circumstances. By choosing the model most relevant to the situation (and modifying it if necessary), we can organise the hypotheses in a meaningful and objective way.

3.4.3   Validate the Model and Make Predictions

Once we've selected a plausible model, we can then focus on validating our choice of hypotheses and model. We do this by gathering new data or by checking the model with existing data. If we're lucky, we may have relevant data from previous research. But often (as we discuss in Chap. 2), market research has been based on a flawed hypothesis and so is at best biased or at worst unusable. We often need to collect new data in a more unbiased way. This ensures that the results reflect the full span of the hypotheses and model that we are testing.

We then use this validated model to decide which factors are important to influence the target behaviour, and in what combination. We can also make predictions and recommendations about what interventions—usually several, not just one—are likely to lead to the targeted behavioural outcomes.

In summary, we've seen that a good behavioural theory is based on hypotheses about what is causing the behaviour. These hypotheses can be measured and tested. When there are several hypotheses about what is causing the behaviour, we need to use an organising model. The model must help us to describe how the behaviour is caused and help to predict future behaviour.

Remember that a model is always 'just' a simplified representation of reality. It does not describe every detail. Reality is complex, but a good model is as simple as possible. Although not complete or perfect, a simplified representation of reality means that we can actually understand and engage with it. A good model makes it possible to explain and account for what you see, for most people, most of the time.

The COM-B and UTAUT are two examples from a wide range of behavioural models available (Michie, Campbell, Brown, West, & Gainforth, 2014b). In some situations, these models do not explain the behaviour well because there are important factors missing. Whether people use a new technology, for example, might be affected by their concerns about privacy infringements. However, even if some important factors are missing, these types of models provide a starting point from which to consider behaviour and can be modified and added to as appropriate.

3.5   WHY SHOULD BUSINESSES USE THEORIES AND MODELS TO MAKE DECISIONS?

Models provide a common language for describing and understanding a situation. If we have a theoretical underpinning about the mental models that people use before we design a product, service or behavioural intervention, there is a much higher chance that we will focus on the aspects that actually influence behaviour.

Using theories and models can save businesses time and money. This is because a theoretical underpinning enables:

- more systematic and rigorous investigation
- navigation of complexity
- more efficient data collection as the focus of the research is known

Let's imagine that you have invented a simple hand-held technology for women. This radical new technology helps them to diagnose the condition of their facial skin and recommends the best skincare and cosmetics products to buy. Let's call it Beauty Advisor. You've put a lot of effort into thinking about how you'd build Beauty Advisor, but you want to test the concept before you go to the trouble of making an expensive prototype.

Typically, you'd commission research to explore women's skincare needs. You'd find out where they currently go to get advice about their skin and find out whether they would pay to buy and use Beauty Advisor. But without some underlying theory about what is likely to influence uptake of your new concept, you may find that you ask the wrong questions, miss out an important component, or focus on the wrong needs.

However, if you use a behavioural model to understand the factors that would cause women to buy and use Beauty Advisor you can quickly focus on what really matters. You can avoid getting distracted by research findings that, although interesting, turn out to be irrelevant to the behaviour you are trying to encourage.

And using this behavioural model may prompt you to add in new features. You might find that it is just as important that Beauty Advisor provides reassurance about a skin condition as it is that it recommends a treatment. The behavioural model helps you to think about the problem more broadly and to build in additional attributes that will help the user to engage better with the product.

Using a model also gives you confidence. You know that when you design your new product, it will have a better chance of success. You have identified the barriers to and promoters of its usage, and you know that you have focussed on addressing only those barriers and promoters that will change a behaviour in the right way.

3.6   SUMMARY

Too many businesses focus on changing attitudes and beliefs rather than on the behaviours themselves. You may want to modify attitudes and beliefs in order to change behaviour, but in the end, you should stay focussed on the behavioural target.

A good theory helps to decide what questions to ask or activities to observe, in order to identify what is really important in influencing behaviour. A model of the behaviour can help to predict future behaviour. If you know which factors really influence behaviour, you can design interventions to change it.

Ultimately, theories of behaviour are fundamental to guiding your decisions about what products and services to design and develop, because they cut through complexity and help you to work out what to focus on.

REFERENCES

Ajzen, I. (1991). The theory of planned behavior. *Organizational Behavior and Human Decision Processes, 50*, 179–211.

Conner, M. (2015). Extending not retiring the theory of planned behaviour: A commentary on Sniehotta, Presseau and Araújo-Soares. *Health Psychology Review, 9*(2), 141–145. https://doi.org/10.1080/17437199.2014.899060

Connor, M., & Armitage, C. J. (1998). Extending the theory of planned behavior: A review and avenues for further research. *Journal of Applied Social Psychology, 28*(15), 1429–1464.

Darnton, A. (2008). *An overview of behaviour change models and their uses* (Government social research: Behaviour change knowledge review). Westminster: Centre for Sustainable Development, University of Westminster.

DiClemente, C. C., & Prochaska, J. O. (1982). Transtheretical Theory: Towards a more integrative theory of change. *Psychotherapy Theory, Research and Practice, 19*(3), 276–287.

Duhigg, C. (2013). *The power of habit: Why we do what we do, and how to change.* Random House Books.

Eltayeb, M., & Dawson, M. (2016). Understanding user's acceptance of personal cloud computing: Using the technology acceptance model. In *Information technology: New generations* (pp. 3–12). Cham: Springer. https://doi.org/10.1007/978-3-319-32467-8_1

Fishbein, M. (1979). Theory of reasoned action. Some applications and implications. *Nebraska Symposium on Motivation, 27*, 65–116.

Fisher, J., Fisher, W., Williams, S., & Malloy, T. (1994). *Empirical tests of an information-motivation-behavioral skills model of AIDS-preventive behavior with gay men and heterosexual university students* (Vol. 13). https://doi.org/10.1037/0278-6133.13.3.238

Gagnon, M. P., Orruño, E., Asua, J., Abdeljelil, A. B., & Emparanza, J. (2012). Using a modified technology acceptance model to evaluate healthcare professionals' adoption of a new telemonitoring system. *Telemedicine Journal and E-Health, 18*(1), 54–59. https://doi.org/10.1089/tmj.2011.0066

Glasman, L. R., & Albarracín, D. (2006). Forming attitudes that predict future behavior: A meta-analysis of the attitude–behavior relation. *Psychological Bulletin, 132*(5), 778–822. https://doi.org/10.1037/0033-2909.132.5.778

Godin, G., & Kok, G. (1996). The theory of planned behavior: A review of its application to health-related behaviors. *American Journal of Health Promotion, 11*(2), 87–98.

Hogg, M. A., & Vaughn, G. M. (2005). *Social psychology* (4th ed.). Essex, UK: Pearson Education Limited.

Holley, C. (2012). *Categorising behavioural characteristics* (HelpDesk Report). DFID. Retrieved from http://www.heart-resources.org/wp-content/uploads/2012/05/Categorising-Behaviourial-Characteristics-February-2012.pdf

Jan, A. U., & Contreras, V. (2011). Technology acceptance model for the use of information technology in universities. *Computers in Human Behavior, 27*(2), 845–851. https://doi.org/10.1016/j.chb.2010.11.009

Michie, S., Atkins, L., & West, R. (2014a). *The behaviour change wheel: A guide to designing interventions.* London: Silverback Publishing.

Michie, S., Campbell, R., Brown, R., West, R., & Gainforth, H. (2014b). *The ABC of behaviour change theories* (1st ed.). London: Silverback Publishing.

Michie, S., van Stralen, M. M., & West, R. (2011). The behaviour change wheel: A new method for characterising and designing behaviour change interventions. *Implementation Science, 6*, 42.

Rogers, E. (1962). *Diffusion of innovations* (1st ed.). New York: Free Press of Glencoe.

Rust, J., & Golombok, S. (2009). *Modern Psychometrics: The Science of Psychological Acceptance* (3rd ed.). London & New York: Routledge.

Sniehotta, F. F., Presseau, J., & Araújo-Soares, V. (2014). Time to retire the theory of planned behaviour. *Health Psychology Review*, *8*(1), 1–7. https://doi.org /10.1080/17437199.2013.869710

St Quinton, T. (2016). Planned behaviour—Stagnation or evolution? *The Psychologist*, *29*, 924–927.

Truong, Y. (2009). An evaluation of the theory of planned behaviour in consumer acceptance of online video and television services. *The Electronic Journal Information Systems Evaluation*, *12*(2), 177–186.

Venkatesh, V., & Davis, F. D. (2000). A theoretical extension of the technology acceptance model: Four longitudinal field studies. *Management Science*, *46*(2), 186–204. https://doi.org/10.1287/mnsc.46.2.186.11926

Venkatesh, V., Morris, M. G., Davis, G. B., & Davis, F. D. (2003). User acceptance of information technology: Toward a unified view. *MIS Quarterly*, *27*(3), 425–478. https://doi.org/10.2307/30036540

The Application of Theory to Intervention Design

Why a Structured Process Is Vital

Abstract To design effective products, services, and interventions, we need to go beyond creativity and gut feel. Rubinstein describes a five-step process that can be applied in business that starts with defining the desired behavioural outcome and takes the reader through approaches for doing a behavioural diagnostic, prioritising the influences on behaviour, identifying suitable behaviour-change techniques, ideating products, services and interventions, and prioritising them, and ends with how to test and evaluate them. The chapter concludes by recommending that the use of a systematic process, grounded in evidence and theory, results in solutions that are more likely to be effective *and* acceptable to the consumer. A structured approach is essential to narrow down to a small number of product and service ideas and interventions that have a higher probability of success.

Keywords Behaviour-change techniques • Behavioural diagnosis • Intervention design • Intervention evaluation

Caroline and Katie were poring over the latest research from Latin America on a nutritional supplement. Their client was trying to understand why so few people were taking it, even though the chronic condition that could be treated by the supplement was increasing and the supplement was readily available and recommended by doctors.

© The Author(s) 2018
H. Rubinstein, *Applying Behavioural Science to the Private Sector*,
https://doi.org/10.1007/978-3-030-01698-2_4

51

To work this out, Caroline and the team had spent several weeks reviewing the client's data and scouring the academic literature to systematically identify a wide range of factors that might contribute to the low use of these supplements. These included barriers: people didn't understand how the supplements could help with their condition, they were forgetting to buy and use them, they were concerned about the cost, and they had a whole range of misperceptions about the condition itself.

The team had been using the data to test their theories and to prioritise the areas to focus on. Many of their hypotheses had been confirmed. For example, the lack of credible and authoritative sources of information was indeed a barrier to uptake. Others had been disproved: cost didn't seem to be a prominent barrier to purchase. In addition, a few new findings emerged—such as the fact that women sometimes reject nutritional supplements because of the unwelcome association with old age.

Armed with this information, it was now clearer which factors needed to be addressed to remove barriers and enhance promoters of uptake.

"*OK,*" said Caroline. "*I'm a chemist. This is not my field of expertise, so I need your help. We have all this data but now we need to get practical. How do we actually work out what are the best types of interventions and how do we have confidence that they could work?*"

Katie, the psychologist, responded. "*It's OK, there's a process for this. We won't just brainstorm a few ideas and then see if they work. We've done the behavioural diagnostic and have a good idea of which factors influence women. If we want women to take these supplements regularly, we will have to work out what categories of behaviour-change activities we should use, identify the right behaviour-change techniques, use these to guide development of plausible interventions, and then test to see if these interventions work.*"

Caroline thought about the conversations she'd been having with the client. "*I'm worried that's going to take a long time, and the client is desperate to see some of our suggested interventions. Can't we just ideate some solutions based on what we already know?*"

"We could," said Katie. *"But believe me, spending a bit more time thinking this through systematically before we start coming up with ideas will save us time and money in the long run. I've done this many time before. However, when we've previously tried to skip important parts of the process, we've had problems."*

* * *

We're now going to discuss this challenge—how we take the theory and data and efficiently generate effective interventions that will help to change behaviour.

Historically, when people have wanted to change behaviour, they designed interventions based on creativity or instinct. They didn't use a behavioural model as a foundation for the interventions and didn't look for evidence that the solutions had worked previously in similar situations. They would jump straight from data collection to intervention design.

The intervention-design process is more than just a creative brainstorm. It should:

- be based on the behavioural diagnosis
- use validated evidence for what works with real people
- select from the full range of behaviour-change techniques that are appropriate to the problem.

Behavioural science is rapidly evolving. There are some good validated approaches to help with this process, such as Intervention Mapping (Bartholomew, Parcel, & Kok, 1998) and the Behaviour-Change Wheel (Michie, Atkins, & West, 2014). The UK Medical Research Council gives guidance on developing and evaluating complex interventions—it advocates drawing on theory in intervention design. However it does not specify how to select and apply the theory (Campbell et al., 2000) (see Chap. 3 for how to select theories).

These approaches differ slightly in the level of detail but in essence they follow the five-step process illustrated in Fig. 4.1. (Chap. 7 is a case study showing how this is used). The process described in this chapter has been developed to fit the needs of the business environment.

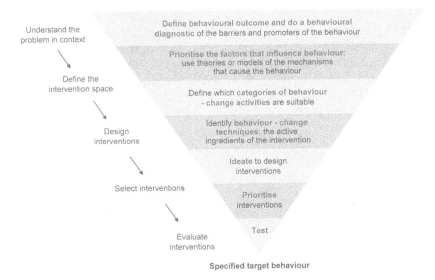

Fig. 4.1   The five steps of intervention design

A good behavioural approach starts with a broad assessment of the behavioural objective and narrows down to a small number of interventions that have a high probability of influencing the behaviour in the desired way. Let's go through each of these five steps in turn.

4.1   Understand the Problem in Context

The starting point is to thoroughly understand the behaviour in context. First you need to precisely define the behaviour you want to change—this is called the *behavioural outcome*—and then conduct a behavioural diagnostic to work out what would be a barrier to achieving the desired outcome or what would promote it.

4.1.1   Define the Behavioural Outcome Before Carrying Out a Behavioural Diagnostic

It may seem obvious, but it is critical that you are precise about exactly what behaviour you are trying to change. Everything you subsequently do will follow from this step. If you are a bit sloppy and get it wrong, you will probably come up with solutions that are ineffective because they are not addressing the right behaviour. It can take more consideration than you might think to correctly define that key behaviour.

For example, if we had just said, 'I want people to take a nutritional supplement regularly,' then we wouldn't know what 'regularly' meant. Once a day? Once a week? We need to be more precise. 'I want people to take a nutritional supplement once a day, one hour before breakfast'. We need to be precise to give more direction and focus to the intervention designer.

Once you have worked out what behaviour you want to encourage, you need to be clear about exactly *whose* behaviour you want to change. Most companies have a lot of information about the target audience for their goods and services, so this step should be straightforward. Again, some degree of specificity is helpful. Do you want women or men to take their nutritional supplements daily, one hour before breakfast? If you are targeting women, should they be 20–30 years of age or older? Is the supplement more important for subpopulations with certain health characteristics, such as women who smoke or women who have an unhealthy diet?

Once you have agreed on the behavioural outcome and the target audience, you need to have a better understanding of *what is influencing* their behaviour. As we have emphasised repeatedly, the behavioural system is complex and many factors interact to cause it, so you need a good 'map' of all the things that influence the behaviour. This is where a behavioural diagnosis is relevant. The COM-B model (described in Chap. 3) is often a good start because it comprehensively maps out a wide range of barriers and promoters of the behaviour. As a reminder, this includes those that are *capabilities* such as knowledge and skills, those that are *opportunities* in the social and physical environment, and those that are *motivations,* both conscious and unconscious.[1] This type of comprehensive analysis ensures that you do not miss out on influences that may be important. There are other frameworks that you could use. For example, the Behavioural

---

[1] Underlying the COM-B is a further classification called the Theoretical Domains Framework (TDF). The TDF comprises 14 domains, and each of these maps on to the COM-B. Below each domain are specific behavioural constructs. For example, under physical capability is the domain of skills. The domain of skills can be further defined as skills development, competence, ability, interpersonal skills, practice and self-assessment (Cane, O'Connor, & Michie 2012, Implementation Science, 7–37). In this way it is possible to make a more detailed diagnosis of the influences on behaviour.

Insights Team developed MINDSPACE, a checklist of the most important influences on behaviour (Dolan, Hallsworth, Halpern, King, & Vlaev, 2010) but it is less comprehensive than COM-B.

The data to conduct the diagnostic may come from several different sources: primary research conducted with the intention of identifying the barriers and promoters, re-analysis of existing data (many companies are sitting on a mountain of research, collected for other purposes, which may contain information that is useful to you) and academic literature or literature in the public domain. It's always better to use the raw material rather than the reports, which may have been curated to confirm existing biases.

Relating to the earlier case study, our client had lots of research documents on people taking nutritional supplements. Additionally, we found a wealth of published literature on people taking or not taking nutritional supplements, especially in the health psychology domain. This type of information helped us to identify themes that occur frequently, and it provided evidence for their importance.

The behavioural diagnostic lists out the wide range of barriers and promoters that might influence a behaviour. This systematic approach allows you to see many possible ways to intervene that you may have otherwise overlooked.

For example, let's think about taking nutritional supplements once a day, one hour before breakfast. You could help people to remember to take the nutritional supplements. You could explain to people why the nutritional supplements are good for them. You could show people how the nutritional supplements work. Or you could do all of those things.

This list of barriers and promoters will reveal many possible ways to influence behaviour. As mentioned before, intervening in several different ways at the same time will be more likely to change behaviour.

4.1.2   Prioritise the Factors You Want to Influence

You will now have an extensive list of the many factors that influence the behaviour you want to change.

In order to prioritise, you need to understand the mechanisms that are behind the behaviour—that is, you want to know how each factor works to change behaviour and how the factors relate to each other to cause the behaviour. This is where an understanding of behavioural models is useful, because the models describe the underlying mechanisms and the contexts in which the behaviours occur.

For example, let's say that the nutritional supplements we want people to take once a day, one hour before breakfast, are good for women who are at risk of a chronic condition. You are looking for a theory that might help you to work out what mechanisms encourage the uptake of supplements to prevent this condition.

Remember that one of the reasons to use a theory (as we have discussed in Chap. 3) is to prioritise and select the best areas for intervention and focus on the mechanisms of the behaviour.

Look for a theory or model to use that could help to explain how different factors work together to cause the behaviour. You may be able to modify the model to better explain the specific behaviour you are investigating.

For example, Protection Motivation Theory (PMT) (Maddux & Rogers, 1983) is a theory that describes how people respond to health threats, and we can apply this to the supplement problem. It is a cognitive model that assumes that decisions are based on two appraisal processes: a threat appraisal and a coping appraisal (see Fig. 4.2). Together, these appraisals result in an intention to take protective action, which in turn

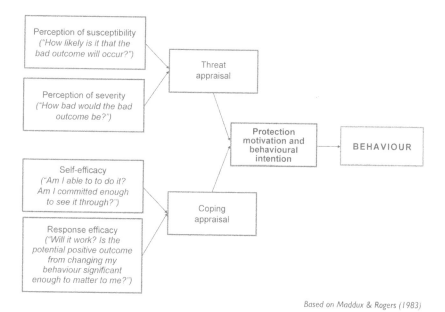

Based on Maddux & Rogers (1983)

Fig. 4.2 Protection Motivation Theory: a theory developed to understand how people respond to health threats

increases protective behaviours. In this case, the protective behaviour is taking a supplement once a day, one hour before breakfast.

You make a threat appraisal based on how severe you perceive the threat to be ("Is getting this condition a serious worry for me?") and whether or not you think you are susceptible to it ("Do I know people in my family that suffer from this condition and if so, could I also get it?"). You make an appraisal of how well you cope based on whether or not you think you are capable of doing something about the threat ("Is it easy for me to get and take these tablets?) and whether or not you believe the solution will be effective in solving the problem ("Is there evidence that these tablets actually work?").

Psychological theories can be quite limited in the mechanisms they specify, so although they help you to focus on areas that are likely to be important, they do not describe everything. For example, the PMT theory does not take account of other influences such as habit or social influence, so you may want to modify it to incorporate other things you found in the behavioural diagnostic. For example, you might discover that social pressure from friends and relatives is a critical factor influencing women to take the nutritional supplement. If this is the case, you could add a factor called 'social norms' to your model that directly influences 'protection motivation' and 'behavioural intention'.

4.2   Define the Intervention Space

Once you've prioritised the factors that influence the behaviour, you need to decide which types of solution are feasible to implement and which should be ruled out.

4.2.1   Define Categories of Behaviour Change Activities

Here, you make a list of all the categories of behaviour change activities that could be used. In the Behaviour-Change Wheel (Michie et al., 2014), nine behaviour-change categories (referred to as intervention functions) are listed including

- education
- persuasion
- incentivisation
- coercion

- training
- enablement (going beyond training, such as surgery to reduce obesity)
- modelling (giving examples of what to aspire to or imitate; demonstrations)
- restructuring the environment
- restrictions

The decision about the types of behaviour-change activities to use is often influenced by company values and principles. Does your company want to take on the job of education? If so, you will be doing this for the general public, not only on behalf of your company, but for the category as a whole. Can your company realistically change the environment of the consumer? Is your company happy to work with partners to achieve an aim, or must you go it alone?

Not all of these options are actually feasible for most organisations. Most companies do not want to coerce or punish people—this is more often the remit of governments, who can impose a sugar tax or fine people for drink-driving. It is also hard for companies to restrict consumers' behaviour. Some companies decide that it is not their role to educate, though they may choose to provide consumers with information to help them make better decisions—like putting information about the source of ingredients on food products. Nevertheless, there are still a variety of interventions that can be used in different situations.

4.2.2   Identify Suitable Behaviour-Change Techniques

So, you've prioritised the factors that affect behaviour, you've defined the intervention space, you've defined the categories of behaviour-change interventions, but you're still not quite ready to design interventions just yet! There is one more step before you can think of specific methods to change your consumers' behaviour—you need to consider all the different techniques that you could use.

These are sometimes referred to as behaviour-change techniques (BCTs). BCTs are the individual 'ingredients' of any intervention (the most basic building block of an intervention) and each BCT is unique. A BCT might involve 'helping someone to set goals', 'encouraging them to reflect on consequences of a behaviour', or 'providing them with information about possible risks'. They are described in this way so as to explain the mechanism for how they work to change behaviour. They form the content of the intervention solutions and can be used alone or in combination with other BCTs.

Using BCTs can help you in two ways. One, there are many BCTs, so you are likely to consider a broader range of solutions. Two, there is often evidence about how effective BCTs are in different situations, so you can select ones that are more likely to be successful.

BCTs have been categorised into many different 'taxonomies,' or option maps. One taxonomy identified 93 individual techniques. Figure 4.3 shows one way of categorising BCTs, in which each cluster contains BCTs that share a common approach.

Each BCT has a formal definition to guide you (Michie et al., 2014). Let's take 'committing to change'—you want people to set new goals and commit to them because when people actively make a commitment to a behaviour they are more likely to do it. The formal definition for this BCT is "Agree on a *clear* and *well-described* behavioural target with a person". Therefore, the solutions you devise could be asking people to agree to a

Goals
Planning and setting goals / Committing to change

Comparison to others
Knowing what people think / Listening to trusted source

Habits
Developing a habit / Swapping a habit / Pairing neutral action with desired behavior / Fading

Surroundings
Adding a prompt / Changing physical surroundings / Changing social influences

Dealing with setbacks
Identifying triggers / Overcorrecting behaviors / Conserving mental resources

Feedback
Framing feedback / Reviewing progress / Monitoring with or without feedback / Monitoring emotional consequences

Informations
Understanding a behavior / Demonstrating a behavior / Knowing the context of the behavior / Knowing about consequences

Identity
'Psyching' yourself up / Thinking about who you are / Thinking about who you could be

Thoughts about change
Reflecting on consequences / Reflecting on pros and cons Reframing / Reflecting on negative consequences / Focusing on past success

Support
Getting support from people / Getting support from things

Rewards and incentives
Promising a reward / Bargaining / Rehearsing future success

Fig. 4.3   Categories of behaviour-change techniques

written 'contract' of behaviour in front of a witness, or affirm or reaffirm their commitment, using statements such as 'I will...".

Remember that the behaviour has to be clear and well-described. In our nutritional supplement example, we would be asking people to commit to:

- taking a tablet in the morning (*action*)
- one hour before breakfast (*context*)
- every day (*frequency*)
- for at least six months (*duration*)
- to prevent the condition (*outcome*)

You know your target behaviour and your target audience, and you've based your intervention objectives on evidence and theory. But how do you select which BCTs to use? Is it a case of trying to fit in as many as possible? No, although you should select a range of BCTs rather than relying on just one or two. You can use your behaviour-change model (as described in step 2) to guide you in selecting which type of BCTs are most appropriate. For example, if your aim is to change attitudes, you should look at BCTs from the categories *information*, and *comparison to others*, and *thoughts about change*.

4.3   IDEATE TO DESIGN INTERVENTIONS

You now know what affects the behaviour, you've looked at the categories of behaviour-change interventions, and you've reviewed the BCTs. The BCTs describe the sort of things you need to do, but you now face the challenge of creatively designing ways to encourage people to perform the specific behaviour that you need—the interventions to influence behaviour.

This stage is often really exciting. However, this means that people frequently jump straight to it without going through the first four steps. In a fast-moving commercial environment, it may seem too time consuming to systematically identify barriers and promoters of the behaviour, build a model that explains why and how the behaviour occurs, or identify behaviour change categories and techniques. After all, there is no peer reviewer who is going to check!

Unfortunately, this can lead to problems. For example, if you have missed out the discussion about the types of BCT to use, you may unintentionally exclude an approach that could be effective. We mentioned earlier that most companies are reluctant to use coercion or restrictions with their consumers. But there may be instances when this could beneficial, as when asking consumers to drink responsibly and not drive. However, if you consider this option you may be able to partner with, and support non-governmental organisations to encourage this behaviour.

You may need to short-cut some steps to speed up the process, but you should try not leave any of them out altogether. You might be able to work in parallel and iterate by starting ideation early and then calibrating against data and evidence as they become available. If you completely cut out steps, you have to base your solutions on *assumptions* about the mechanisms that are causing the behaviour. If you go straight from data collection to intervention design, for example, you are likely to design interventions that focus on the wrong things, because you haven't understood why a behaviour occurs. It is often a false economy to jump to the design phase before you thoroughly understand what needs to happen for behaviour change to occur.

When designing interventions, it's useful to have several different people contributing to the creative process. Diverse viewpoints are important. Invite people who may bring an interesting and different perspective as well as those who have been immersed in the problem on a daily basis. If you were trying to design interventions about supplement uptake, for example, you might want to include someone from marketing, someone who knows the retail environment, someone who understands the biological effects of taking the supplements, a behavioural scientist, and a designer. The benefits and challenges of multidisciplinary methods of working are discussed in Chap. 6.

We've discussed how to get to the creative process, and who should contribute, but the next stage is the creative intervention-design process itself. There are many different ways to conduct this process (VanGundy, 2008) and many books on this topic, but these are not discussed here. The process should be structured to address those factors in the behaviour-change model that influence the desired behaviour. When you generate ideas, you need to keep the BCTs and theoretical framework in mind. Exactly how you execute the interventions and bring them to life is the creative part, but you need to keep linking your ideas back to the behavioural diagnosis and the theoretical models. Every time a new idea is generated, ask yourself these questions:

- what determinant(s) of behaviour is this idea addressing?
- what is the mechanism or process by which this will change behaviour?

This doesn't detract from any of the creative process, but it does ensure that your creative ideation is grounded in theory and evidence.

4.4   PRIORITISE INTERVENTIONS

By this stage, your team will have generated lots of interventions that may change behaviour. Now, you need to prioritise the interventions that are most likely to be effective.

To do this, you need some criteria by which to evaluate each idea. The initial selection tends to rely on judgment and the needs of the business. When we were designing interventions for increasing nutritional uptake, we considered the following criteria:

- is there evidence that this has worked previously?
- does the intervention fit the brand?
- can we afford to create the intervention in a reasonable time scale?
- do we think it will work? For example, will people be more willing to engage with pharmacists to ask for the supplement? Will they take the tablets according to the instructions on the pack?
- could there be unintended consequences or impacts on company reputation?

Each behaviour-change situation will require a different set of criteria. Frequently, these criteria are implicit during the design process, but at this stage, you need to make them explicit so you can select suitable interventions.

There are different methods to select the best intervention solutions. One, used by the authors of the Behaviour-Change Wheel (Michie et al., 2014), is called 'APPEASE'. It ranks solutions on affordability, practicality, effectiveness and cost-effectiveness, acceptability, side-effects and safety, and equity.

Another selection method is to place the interventions on a risk–reward chart (Fig. 4.4). A risk–reward chart assesses the interventions on two dimensions: how positive the outcome will be (reward) and how much risk there is to the implementation. In this way, we can compare several

Intervention evaluation

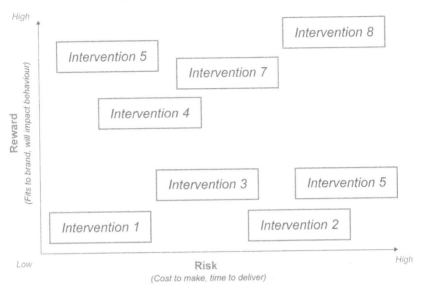

Fig. 4.4   Intervention evaluation: risk–reward analysis for nutritional supplement example

interventions against each other to work out if it is worth taking a risk to gain the expected reward. Although this approach can be somewhat subjective, it still helps to identify an initial set of interventions to test.

To plot a risk–reward chart that is useful for your specific situation, you need to decide on the most appropriate axes. For the supplements case, we defined a high-reward intervention as one that fitted well with the brand and was very likely to affect consumer behaviour. We defined a high-risk intervention as one that was expensive to deliver or time-consuming to develop.

Once you've designed the chart, you can then plot your interventions. In Fig. 4.4 interventions 4, 5, and 7 cluster at the high reward and low risk end of the chart. These look promising. Interventions 2 and 6 are low reward and high risk, and so are rejected. Interventions 1 and 3 are low risk and low reward and so are also rejected because they will have too little impact. Intervention 8 is high reward but high risk—rather than outright rejection, it needs further consideration.

High-reward, low-risk interventions can usually deliver value quickly. High-reward, high-risk interventions, such as intervention 8, may require more time to develop and refine, so may be more suitable as part of a longer-term development strategy to be investigated at a later stage.

Sometimes an intervention is only effective when combined with another. For example, providing information about consequences (Intervention 3) may be less effective on its own but when combined with seeing a video of a person modelling the behaviour (Intervention 4), it might be much more effective in changing behaviour. This means that the selection and prioritisation process must be collaborative and discursive, encouraging the intervention designers to reflect on why they are selecting one intervention rather than another. In this way, you avoid the problem identified at the beginning of this chapter—of designing interventions based only on creativity and gut feel alone.

4.5   Test and Evaluate

Once you've generated many different ideas and prioritised those that have most potential, you then need to test and evaluate them.

The testing methods you choose depends on the type of intervention. Is it simple or complex? Are you evaluating a single intervention or a full behaviour-change programme that incorporates several interventions? Are you testing a physical product or a digital offering?

For example, if you want to know whether a change to the way a description of a product affects people's willingness to use the product, you could conduct a simple online test where you compare one version of the description against another.

But if you were testing a more complex behaviour-change programme, for example, to encourage people not to drink and drive, you may want to select several test methods. You may want to assess the acceptability of the interventions with customers in a bar by doing interviews *and* the effectiveness of the interventions in preventing drink-driving by doing an exit survey.

With the data you collect from these tests, you will want to evaluate how effective the interventions were. There are three categories of evaluation. You can evaluate

- the *outcome* (does it work? how well?)
- *cost-effectiveness* (is it value for money?)
- the *process* (how it worked and for whom?)

Table 4.1   Examples of different approaches to evaluation

	Outcome evaluation	Process evaluation	Cost effectiveness
Example test methods	A–B testing Randomised controlled trial	'Think-aloud' interviews Ethnographic research observing products in use	Cost estimation Return-on-investment model

The methods you use will vary according to what you are evaluating (Table 4.1).

If you want to know whether an intervention delivered the desired outcome, for example, you might want to conduct A–B testing, where two versions of an intervention are compared to see which one performs better. This is very commonly used for digital interventions where two variants, A and B, are shown to similar users at the same time.

Or you may want to perform some form of randomised controlled trial (RCT), where one group is shown the intervention and a matched group is not. If you find that significantly more people in the group with the intervention perform the desired behaviour, the intervention has been a success.

If you want to evaluate the process, it may be better to use 'think-aloud' techniques, where you ask users to articulate their thoughts as they use an intervention, a part of an intervention, or a mock-up of an intervention. You can also conduct ethnographic research and observe people and record their behaviour as they interact with an intervention.

To evaluate cost effectiveness, you need to assess the costs of implementing the intervention against the likely benefits. One way to do this is to build a spreadsheet model that uses the predicted effect size[2] of the interventions to calculate the expected return on investment (ROI). Typically, there is no prior data for this, so you may have to base your calculations on analogous situations. For example, if you had no prior information about interventions to encourage the purchase and daily use of nutritional supplements, you might look for other situations where interventions for health or nutrition have been targeted at women in the same age group in the same country. You can then use the reported outcomes or effect sizes to calculate an estimated ROI. This means that you will have to make assumptions to overcome gaps in the data, but it may be better than being unable to evaluate your decisions.

It can be tempting to omit this final stage of testing and evaluation. Some people design interventions and then roll them out wholesale, but

---

[2] In statistics, an effect size is a standardised measure of the magnitude of a phenomenon.

this means that interventions may be ineffective, costly, or both. Including a test and evaluation stage in the behaviour-change programme helps you to learn what works and what doesn't. You can then use this knowledge to modify and create better interventions in the future.

In an ideal world, this testing process would be rigorous and iterative, involving multiple cycles and development before the tested ideas are ready for implementation. This allows you to change the interventions, so you know that they are effective.

But if you do not have sufficient time to do this, it is worth trying to find rapid 'test-learn-adapt' methods. For example, conduct concept testing with a small group of consumers at an early stage—even when the interventions are not finalised—to provide input to further development.

4.6   SUMMARY

Interventions are more likely to succeed if they are

- grounded in theory
- effective in similar situations
- designed and selected using a rigorous, evidence-based process.

In the absence of theory and an evidence base, people tend to repeat the mistakes of their predecessors or apply interventions that are not relevant or cannot be effective.

If you want to develop products, services, or interventions that are likely to influence consumer behaviour, you should follow a systematic process: understand the problem in context, define the intervention space, design interventions, select those with most potential and then test and evaluate them.

Ultimately this process is more likely to ensure that the intervention solutions you design have a greater possibility of success in encouraging the behaviour change you want to see.

REFERENCES

Bartholomew, L. K., Parcel, G. S., & Kok, G. (1998). Intervention mapping: A process for developing theory- and evidence-based health education programs. *Health Education & Behavior: The Official Publication of the Society for Public Health Education, 25*(5), 545–563. https://doi.org/10.1177/10901981980 2500502

Campbell, M., Fitzpatrick, R., Haines, A., Kinmonth, A. L., Sandercock, P., Spiegelhalter, D., & Tyrer, P. (2000). Framework for design and evaluation of complex interventions to improve health. *BMJ, 321*(7262), 694–696. https://doi.org/10.1136/bmj.321.7262.694

Cane, J., O'Connor, D., & Michie, S. (2012). Validation of the theoretical domains framework for use in behaviour change and implementation research. *Implementation Science, 7*(1), 37.

Dolan, P., Hallsworth, M., Halpern, D., King, D., & Vlaev, I. (2010). *MINDSPACE: Influencing behaviour through public policy.* Cabinet Office; Institute for Government. Retrieved from http://38r8om2xjhhl25mw24492dir.wpengine.netdna-cdn.com/wp-content/uploads/2015/07/MINDSPACE.pdf

Maddux, J. E., & Rogers, R. W. (1983). Protection motivation and self-efficacy: A revised theory of fear appeals and attitude change. *Journal of Experimental Social Psychology, 19*(5), 469–479.

Michie, S., Atkins, L., & West, R. (2014). *The behaviour change wheel: A guide to designing interventions.* London: Silverback Publishing.

VanGundy, A. B. (2008). *101 activities for teaching creativity and problem solving.* John Wiley & Sons.

PART II

Embedding Behavioural Science in the Business

The first part of this book focussed on the theory of behavioural science and its relevance to commercial issues. The second half describes how to put this theory into practice. How can behavioural science be used in a business? What type of business activities is it best suited to? And what are the challenges of introducing this new discipline into organisations that have well-developed ways of doing things?

Chapter 5 explores the integration of behavioural science into business and how companies can overcome resistance to its introduction and use. It is a case study of how behavioural science was introduced into an established business, what the challenges were to its integration, and what lessons were learned. The chapter highlights the potential fears, concerns, and confusion that must be addressed to ensure successful integration. It describes how behavioural science is not suited for all challenges and how the organisation needs to be clear about where and how it adds value. It explains the need for behavioural-science 'champions' within the organisation and the importance of a credible, experienced team leader, who can explain why this approach to understanding human behaviour is more valuable than more conventional methods.

Chapter 6 describes how to make behavioural science work in multidisciplinary teams. Not only is behavioural science effective as part of a multidisciplinary team, its applications are so wide ranging that it is more likely than many disciplines to be used in this way. Many functions touch on the way people interact with each other and with products and services. This chapter provides a brief overview of the academic literature on the benefits and challenges of working in multidisciplinary teams and describes a case study of how this works in practice. It lays out guidelines for making multidisciplinary teamworking effective. These guidelines include how to build trust, manage professional identities, cope with different communication styles, manage uncertainty, deal with complexity, assess quality, deal with time pressures and availability, and the role of the leader.

Chapter 7 is a case study of using behavioural science in practice with Southwest Airlines. It shows how behavioural science was applied to improve the boarding experience at the airport gate in ways that satisfied the needs of passengers, employees, and the business. This chapter describes how the principles for applying behavioural science described in Chap. 4 were used to address the challenge. It summarises the activities that enabled the development of a model of passenger behaviour and shows the application of the five-step approach to intervention design. It ends by revealing some of the solutions that were devised and describes the results of a testing programme in a US airport.

Chapter 8 discusses the ethical risks for behavioural science. It describes the power of the behavioural science approach and why there should be guidelines to ensure that it is used ethically. The chapter outlines the debate about the ethics of nudging in the public sector where, despite being used to promote good behaviour, it has been accused of 'soft paternalism' and the removal of free choice. It argues that, although people are suspicious of its use in the private sector, there is a precedent for self-regulation and good use. It explains why behavioural science in the private sector does not have to be deceitful, covert, or manipulative, and how the consumer–company relationship differs from the citizen–policy-maker relationship. It suggests five guidelines to help practitioners make better, more ethical decisions.

Chapter 9 is about the value of applying behavioural science in the private sector. It describes how managers in consumer-facing and business-to-business sectors can get value from its application, and how students of psychology and business can learn to apply behavioural theory to real-world problems. This chapter reprises the main themes of the book. First, if businesses apply the scientific method to understanding consumers and customers, they are more likely to know what is really driving behaviour, and hence be able to design products, services and interventions that better meet people's needs. Second, using a structured, evidence-based approach helps to navigate complexity and saves time and money in the long run. Finally, incorporating behavioural science into a commercial organisation can be highly beneficial if the company is clear about how it will add value and has a plan for how to introduce it.

CHAPTER 5

The Integration of Behavioural Science into Business

How to Overcome Resistance to Using It in the Organisation

Abstract This is a case study of how behavioural science was introduced into an established business, the challenges of integrating it and the lessons learned for how to apply it. Rubinstein highlights the importance of addressing the concern that behavioural science will disrupt tried and tested ways of working, and the need to change internal mindsets. Behavioural science is not suited for all challenges and the organisation needs to be clear about where and how it adds value. If a company decides to develop a behavioural science function, it is necessary to identify a senior manager to champion the new function and find a leader with behavioural science expertise who can communicate, build and lead a team of specialists. The leader needs to make the case for why using the scientific method to understand human behaviour is more effective than existing approaches.

Keywords Innovation • Leadership • Resistance to change • Team building

© The Author(s) 2018
H. Rubinstein, *Applying Behavioural Science to the Private Sector*,
https://doi.org/10.1007/978-3-030-01698-2_5

Ben, Alastair, Colin and Geraint were sitting in the main boardroom at Innovia in August 2014, discussing the induction plan for the new senior hire who was joining the company in four weeks' time.

"It'll be good to have a consultant with a background in psychology on the team," Geraint commented. *"We'll be working with someone who really has in-depth expertise in human motivation and behaviour."*

Alastair agreed. *"Going deeper into psychology might help us to design products and services that really meet people's needs and desires."*

Ben looked uncomfortable. As the head of the design team, he thought that the designers were already pretty good at understanding people's needs. *"I hope she shows us new ways to do things,"* he said.

Colin nodded. *"Judging from her CV, she will have some new approaches. However, we really need to make sure that she fully understands how we work and is properly integrated into the team."*

"It's always a challenge when we introduce a new function here," Alastair said. *"But we have done it before successfully and as long as we give her time to explain what she does and how she does it, I think we'll be OK."*

And so, it was. This chapter is about how the new discipline of behavioural science was introduced to Innovia and how it became integrated into Innovia's multi-disciplinary culture.

* * *

In earlier chapters, we discussed the history of behavioural science, saw how theories and models can be used to improve research and refine product and service design, and described a process for designing interventions to change behaviour. This chapter is a case study of how behavioural science was introduced into a well-established company—Innovia Technology, where I work today. We'll cover the challenges that we faced around integration, and the opportunities that we found to apply it well. Along the way, we'll see real-life examples of how behavioural science was used to good effect. We'll cover the challenges of introduction, how we gained credibility, and then how we generalised our findings to other companies.

We introduced behavioural science into Innovia Technology, a company that specialises in 'front-end' innovation. This is the type of innovation that occurs very early on in the design of products and services—well before the commercial phase of new product development (Koen, Bertels, & Kleinschmidt, 2014). To innovate well at this early stage, you need a 'holistic' approach (one that crosses organisational disciplines) and you need to be comfortable with high levels of uncertainty (Herstatt & Verworn, 2001; Khurana & Rosenthal, 1998). The methods and approaches used at this stage of new business creation are different from the more typical type of everyday incremental innovation, because you are trying to imagine and design new concepts that may differ radically from what has gone before (Val-Jauregi & Justel, 2007). Not surprisingly, this stage is often referred to as 'the fuzzy front end'. It rarely follows a linear trajectory. You need to be comfortable with high levels of ambiguity, to be able to learn and iterate, and you also need huge amounts of patience!

Innovia Technology was founded in Cambridge, UK in 1999. At the time of writing, the company consists of a group of about eighty people with a wide range of backgrounds—physics, chemistry, engineering, product and industrial design, psychology, biology, public health, biochemistry, and veterinary science. They operate in a large, open-plan space—there are no departments or divisions. Biologists sit next to engineers, and chemists with designers. Innovian material scientists work seamlessly on project teams with biochemists and economists, solving innovation challenges for some of the world's largest and most successful companies— Shell, Procter & Gamble, PepsiCo, Boeing, LEGO and Bayer. Many of their innovations have resulted in the granting of worldwide patents for their clients. Innovia consultants most frequently interact with people in Research and Development, Innovation, Marketing, and Strategy departments.

Up until 2014, however, there were no psychologists in the company, even though many of the challenges they worked on had a human component. Instead, there were talented individuals who had developed a good feel for end users. So, for example, they found a way to convincingly demonstrate to consumers the benefits of contact lenses for astigmatism that was far better than the conventional Snellen chart; they designed a strapless bra, using engineering principles, which was a hit with consumers; and they created a world-record setting swimsuit, in part informed by research into swimmer psychology. This broad experience helped many of the consultants to develop some degree of intuition.

Nevertheless, Innovia recognised that experience and intuition are not easily scaled, can be subjective, and may be incorrect. To improve services further, Innovia decided to bring in someone with expert knowledge of how people think, feel and behave. In September 2014, I joined Innovia as the only psychologist in the company. My background was varied. I had worked in market research and advertising and had run a global brand consultancy. I had a doctorate in social psychology and had conducted research in health psychology. I felt ready for a new challenge in the world of innovation and was convinced that the behavioural sciences could play an important role in the development of better products and services. But, to make this possible, I needed to develop an approach that would fit with the established ways of working at the firm.

Taking on a behavioural scientist was an experiment for the company. Four years on, Innovia would say that the experiment has been a resounding success. Behavioural scientists with backgrounds in social and health psychology, consumer psychology, behavioural economics, experimental design and cognitive neuroscience are now part of the team. Within the multidisciplinary teams, our behavioural scientists create even more value for companies working at the front end of innovation. What follows is a description of how it was introduced and integrated into the organisation.

5.1   What Are the Challenges with Integrating Behavioural Science into an Organisation?

I asked ten senior innovation consultants at Innovia to describe their experience of this integration process. Specifically, they discussed how they felt when each new set of skills in behavioural science was first introduced in the company, how easy or difficult it was to integrate it into operations, and what were the successes and failures. As all of these consultants work closely with client companies, I wanted to know what they perceived to be the biggest barriers faced by large corporations when trying to use behavioural science and where the capability fits most easily within a company.

From this, I identified three major barriers to the integration of behavioural science.

1. Fear of disrupting tried-and-tested ways of working
2. Concern about effectiveness of the approach
3. Confusion about why this approach is different

5.1.1   Fear of Disrupting Tried-and-Tested Ways of Working

As with many human responses to change, although the rationale for employing people with expertise in understanding behaviour was very logical, the response to change was more emotional. People worried that this new approach might disrupt their usual ways of working.

Shreyas, an innovation strategist, commented that, *"People didn't know what behavioural science was. Why would it be beneficial? How would it be different from what we traditionally do?"*

Geraint, one of the founders of Innovia, reflected that there were concerns that it would somehow disrupt the usual way of working. *"We had established ways of solving problems that needed people insight—then behavioural science came along and we had to change our expectations of what tools we needed to use."*

This is not unique to behavioural science; there may be resistance to change when any new way of doing things is introduced into a system that is already working efficiently. When there is no apparent problem, people want business as usual. But with behavioural science, this problem is often compounded by a lack of institutional knowledge about what methods it used, and confusion about how it differs from other activities that sounded similar.

People can find it hard to understand the unique benefits that behavioural science provides. Ben, the head of design, thought that it might be similar to design thinking, which focuses on peoples' needs. Alex, who led the life scientists, wondered whether it was really just the same as the consumer-insight work he'd done before. Rob, the head of sales, said it sounded similar to what the marketing people did.

As Ben later reflected, *"Innovia needed behavioural science to improve our understanding of peoples' needs and motivations but we had to be careful in how we positioned it. There was a buzz around behavioural science and we had to get people up to speed in a soft way. It's a perfect fit for both the techies and the creatives here, but there were tensions in both camps."*

Bringing in a new capability can be difficult for the organisation. As with any scientific discipline, people trained in behavioural science have particular ways of approaching problems, and these approaches are not familiar to everyone. People have to learn each other's languages. Fortunately, Innovia was better placed than many companies to overcome these barriers.

As Alastair, the CEO, said, *"being curious, diverse, and holistic are core to the way we work. People take that very seriously and so we accept more learning pain than most would. We think it is worth going through because it is the right way to operate. We support each other rather than laughing at each other."*

5.1.2   Concern About the Effectiveness of the Approach

As befits those who work at the fuzzy front end of innovation, Innovians are open-minded. Although they had reservations about how behavioural science might contribute, they were prepared to see how it could help. An opportunity came along early: a project about wet shaving for males in Asia. This needed both an understanding of the technical effects of shaving and an understanding of the consumer—a truly multidisciplinary problem.

Innovia's new behavioural science process meant that it approached the challenge in a very different way than it had approached previous challenges.

- The team used a model of consumer behaviour (an adapted version of the Theory of Planned Behaviour (Ajzen, 1991)) to identify the most important factors influencing shaving behaviour
- The team populated the model with the client's existing data, so didn't need to collect new data
- The insights derived from this analysis led to communications that focussed on the benefits of wet shaving to the skin
- Interventions to increase wet shaving were designed based on an understanding of how habits are created

The behavioural scientists helped to translate technical data into meaningful communications for the consumers. The designers then brought these communications to life. The behavioural scientists ensured that the communication strategies were evidence-based and facilitated the knowledge transfer from the technical rationale to the consumer communications.

The behavioural scientists certainly demonstrated how they could contribute to front-end innovation. This project proved that this new method of working was relevant and led to different ways to communicate with consumers.

There was a degree of beginner's luck here. Not every subsequent project was as straightforward. The shaving project had lots of existing data, but this isn't always the case. We can't do an analysis or a behavioural diagnostic without data—otherwise we would have to rely on intuition and hunches. Data gathering can be expensive and time consuming. Even with good input data, the process of designing an effective intervention (as described in Chap. 4) takes more time than just going straight from the behavioural diagnostic to intervention design. In line with the scientific method, there may be several rounds of testing and evaluation: we may decide to test hypotheses about the model of behaviour, and we may test the interventions to see if they are effective in changing behaviour. As Kora, a behavioural economist, commented, *"there is a tension between using the scientific approach and being quick".*

It's important to be rigorous, but in a commercial context, it's also important to deliver solutions in a timely fashion. The five-step process, described in Chap. 4 was developed, in part, to show how to address behavioural challenges in a systematic way but also to show how to flex as the challenge requires.

5.1.3   Confusion About Why This Approach Is Different

Initially, Innovians did not know what behavioural science was. They needed to understand when they should use behavioural science on projects, and they needed to be involved in the behavioural science process so they understood the value that it could deliver. People could then see how different it was from the market research and consumer insights they had previously been exposed to.

Shreyas thought that behavioural science as a separate discipline was hard for people to understand because *"a lot of evidence is counter-intuitive. People make assumptions [about why people do things] and believe they are intuitive about other people. We all have biases. Everyone is human and everyone behaves. Therefore, everyone thinks that they are experts on human behaviour."*

Differentiating behavioural science was therefore really important. It was not just a case of educating people about the benefits of using behavioural science. People also needed to understand why it's hard to understand human behaviour intuitively. They needed to change their mindset from 'I understand human behaviour because I am human' to 'It's really hard to predict human behaviour and very difficult to change it!' This message was not only important for Innovians, but also for our clients.

Tim, a physicist by training, summarised the challenge in this way. *"You sometimes get pushback against looking at the problem with different eyes. It's hard to innovate if you don't really understand people. Behavioural science has an exploratory power that is not just descriptive—you can extrapolate from it. Marketing insights are OK if you want to interpolate, but in breakthrough innovation we can't just interpolate because we have to move away from where we are now."*

5.2   HOW DID BEHAVIOURAL SCIENCE QUICKLY BUILD CREDIBILITY?

Over the next few years, the new behavioural science capability gained credibility within Innovia and with its clients. This integration and acceptance were successful for four major reasons: the scientific method fitted the culture and approaches already in use; it was well communicated and explained; the team was experienced and knowledgeable; and, critically, the approach was aligned with the objectives and values of the business. These are described in more detail below.

5.2.1   It Used the Scientific Method

Innovia, as a consultancy with a strong foundation in science and technology, was sympathetic to an approach that used the scientific method. The rigorous behavioural science approach was a natural fit in a culture that was suspicious of approaches that were 'soft and unsubstantiated' and it worked very well with breakthrough innovation.

"It helped us to think about what shaped human behaviour, including irrationality, in a rational way," said Rob.

Tim echoed this thought. *"It's not a black box. You can explain this to technical clients and say what it is for."*

5.2.2   It Was Well Communicated and Explained

To help people understand the value of this approach, I had to develop a clear strategy to explain to people at Innovia what behavioural science was and what were the benefits of using it. My explanation needed to be simple enough to understand but detailed enough to show how behavioural science differed from traditional methods of understanding the consumer.

When people asked, I said, *"Have you ever noticed that people don't always do what they say they do? Can you see the problem with collecting research where you ask people what they do, and then assume they will actually do that? With behavioural science, you don't need to think about what people say they do, you can just focus on what they actually do."* Andy, a physicist and relationship manager, found this particularly helpful in trying to work out when and why to use behavioural science on projects. *"'Why don't people do what they say they do?' I got that really quickly and it made sense."*

I had a quick explanation for people who asked me about behavioural science, but I also needed to reach the people who didn't ask me. I organised a series of company-wide learning sessions to explain the approaches and processes that could be used, taking care to demonstrate their practical applicability wherever possible.

Alastair reflected that, *"it was both difficult and easy to take on board. We realised how poorly we understood what to do to influence behaviour and how unsuccessful our attempts often are. Going deeper into psychology might help to solve these problems in the real world. So, we recognised that it could help us to understand how our brains worked."*

5.2.3   The Team Was Experienced and Knowledgeable

It was an advantage that I had a credible background spanning both the commercial sector and the academic world. I had a lot of knowledge from my professional commercial experience, but I was also up-to-date with the latest academic thinking. More importantly, I recruited a diverse team to help us to apply behavioural science effectively across a wide range of projects.

In keeping with Innovia's belief in the importance of working in holistic teams, the behavioural scientists were also holistic: their backgrounds spanned social psychology, health psychology, psychobiology, cognitive neuroscience, experimental psychology, behavioural economics, and consumer psychology. And just as chemists had to learn to understand the language of the engineers, the behavioural scientists had to learn to speak each other's language. It may surprise those outside the discipline of psychology that social psychologists are trained quite differently from neuroscientists, who in turn are trained differently from behavioural economists. There is a common base, but as they progress through their discipline-specific training, their approaches diverge.

Our response to this was to build the identity of the team. Behavioural science is a relatively new discipline, at least in its current form, and so we needed the team to share some core approaches and speak the same language. To achieve this, we designed a training course with a core curriculum to be used for our new joiners.

5.2.4   The Approach Was Aligned with Business Objectives and Values

It should seem obvious, but it is unlikely that a new capability or approach will be embraced unless it can meet the company's objectives and fit with its values. In the case of Innovia, senior managers believed that integrating behavioural science would contribute to the fundamental business objective of developing breakthrough innovation that really made a difference to clients and to the consumer experience. They also saw that it could be a platform for business growth for Innovia. Right from the start, there was clarity that behavioural science could add value.

As Emma, a psychobiologist, said, *"think about why you want to use it. What is it for? Use behavioural science when you want non-trivial behaviour changes, such as when you want to develop an innovative product or service."*

It is much easier to use a new approach if it fits with your values. Behavioural science fitted well with the way that Innovia tackled innovation challenges in general: combining the rigorous scientific approach with creativity and using holistic teams to deliver solutions.

Alastair commented that, *"when we founded Innovia, it was an article of faith that holistic working is better, but we really had to demonstrate it. In fact, we actually see it in good results all the time."*

Without these conditions, it would have been much more difficult to socialise the discipline into the company.

5.3   HOW CAN THESE LEARNINGS BE GENERALISED TO OTHER COMPANIES?

At the same time as our Innovia consultants were working out how to use behavioural science, people in corporations were also facing the same challenge. In 2014, it was still a relatively new approach and people were interested to find out more. By 2018, most people had heard about behavioural science—Kahneman and Tversky's work had been popularised

(Lewis, 2017), Kahneman's own book, Thinking Fast and Slow, had been top of the bestseller lists (Kahneman, 2012), and Richard Thaler had won a Nobel Prize for behavioural economics.

It wasn't just Innovia's employees who had encountered challenges in applying behavioural science at the coalface of business. Many of the challenges faced by other organisations seemed to be similar to those experienced at Innovia. Some departments thought it was simply another way to do what they did.

"Marketing departments can be particularly resistant," said Geraint. *"It looks strange and may seem in conflict with what they already know."*

Rob, a physicist who had spent some time working in a large oil company, found that *"engineers can see it as fluffy and irrelevant. Engineers feel like they take rational business decisions and assume people follow systems."*

Habits are hard to break. Departments have tried-and-tested beliefs and approaches. As Tim commented, *"these approaches are good, but mostly were developed before we understood how to apply behavioural science to business problems."*

Even those companies that are more open to the idea of using behavioural science had encountered problems. Alex recalled that one company in the pharmaceutical sector had been trying to recruit behavioural scientists but didn't know the best place to find them. They asked us, *"should they be looking for people with a background in research or psychology and if so, what type of psychology?"* They had some difficulty in finding the right type of individual with the right skills to fit into the business.

Ben found that his clients were starting to be concerned that there were 'charlatans' who say they do behavioural science but in fact did not have qualifications in the discipline—they were claiming to apply behavioural science because it was 'in vogue'. *"It is hard to work out if you are getting value. How do you assess value?"*

The biggest challenge that had emerged was where to put behavioural science in an organisation. Who has the remit to embrace and own it?

Alastair thought that, *"big companies are often organised in silos and may not get good results unless they can integrate behavioural science across the company."*

One big question is whether behavioural science should be a new function in marketing, or an asset to R&D? Is there a role for behavioural science in the HR department? Is it better suited to the consumer-insights team? Or could it be useful to data scientists? What if it were a separate department that could be a service to other departments? There are clearly pros and cons to all these options.

Tim was concerned about integration. *"If it is a separate department, people don't think it is for them and don't take responsibility."*

Geraint went a step further. *"Perhaps it should be seen as really a methodology rather than a department. In ten years' time, people will see it as important."*

One theme emerged particularly strongly: the ability of behavioural science to bridge the divide between marketing and R&D. Traditionally, R&D teams develop new products and services usually from a technical perspective. They can be frustrated that marketing teams don't seem to understand the technology or ask for a new product or service that is technically impossible. Marketing teams are equally frustrated that R&D teams don't seem to understand what is relevant to consumers and so they make their products too complex to use. In a sense, behavioural scientists can speak both languages: they can provide a systematic look at what is driving behaviour, using a scientific method that technical experts can appreciate, *and* they can provide insights into the deep underlying motivations behind consumer behaviour that marketing teams find so valuable.

As Geraint reflected *"Needing to have a bridge between R&D and marketing is not new. Behavioural science is both behaviour AND science so you can build a bridge that others can't"*.

5.4   When Should You Use Behavioural Science? When Shouldn't You?

Behavioural science is not suited for all challenges. It does not, and should not, replace well-tried, effective techniques that are already in use. Behavioural science is especially suited to complex problems where other approaches have not been able to go deep enough into the drivers of behaviour. Below are some examples of where behavioural science is appropriate.

- You are developing a new technology and there is little knowledge of how people might respond. For example, you want to understand how people will interact with autonomous vehicles (see Box 5.1)
- You are seeking to break a deeply embedded habit or change a complex behaviour where more conventional approaches have been unsuccessful. For example, you need to persuade people that they should not drive after having an alcoholic drink.

- You want to change internal behaviours in the organisation and need a more systematic method to diagnose the barriers to implementing a new approach. For example, you are trying to encourage the uptake of a new technology across the entire company that will require new capabilities and different responses.
- There is a need for a completely fresh perspective and richer understanding to encourage people to think about a challenge in a different and more radical way. This may be even more important when the traditional approach already *seems* effective, so people just do what they have always done. For example, you need to make boarding a plane a pleasant experience whilst at the same time ensuring that it is quick.

5.5   SUMMARY

The decision of how best to use behavioural science and where the discipline should be in the company will clearly depend on the specific needs of the individual organisation. But to have a chance of success, consider these criteria:

- Think about what you want to use it for: it is not a panacea and is better for some challenges than others
- Find a champion within the company (preferably at a senior level) who can ensure that it is integrated, understood, implemented, and embraced
- Think carefully about what sort of behavioural scientist you need in the corporation: make sure they have a background in the behavioural and psychological sciences that they know how to apply, and that they are credible commercially to colleagues
- Take the effort to communicate to key stakeholders the value of what it does, how it does it, and how it differs from other tried-and-tested approaches
- Adapt and integrate behavioural science into existing approaches to ensure both rigour and timeliness. Avoid siloing at all costs because behavioural science really comes into its own in combination with other functions

Box 5.1 Using Behavioural Science for an Innovation Challenge
Innovia Technology has addressed these types of challenge in the context of their approach to breakthrough innovation. Their approach is a simple but intuitive one that can be divided into three broad phases, known in the company as Understand, Explore, Decide (UED).

The **Understand** phase. Here, the problem is defined, broken down, and reassembled. This is a fuzzy process but is the most critical part of the three phases, and often takes the most time. The aim is to create a framework that encapsulates the insights from the understand phase. This framework helps us to innovate and can be used when we explore solutions. The innovation framework provides a route to creating ideas, and can be a simple model, taxonomy, or a breakdown of the problem into component parts (problem areas). The solar road studs project described in Chap. 1 is a good example of how a behavioural science theory provided a framework from which we could explore solutions.

The **Explore** phase is designed to open up possibilities. Here, we investigate the problem areas and create ideas to solve them using insights from different situations, companies and people. These ideas are then turned into new concepts to address the real problem defined during the understand phase. At this stage, there may be many different ideas that might result in an effective solution. Behavioural science can be useful to explore the possibilities from a psychological perspective. For example, we ran a programme for Southwest Airlines (discussed in detail in Chap. 7) that was designed to improve the boarding experience. We developed hypotheses based on our knowledge of the psychology of waiting and queuing and how people plan (or don't plan) ahead. This enabled us to design a wide range of effective solutions that were acceptable and enjoyable to the passengers, but also made the boarding process much quicker.

The **Decide** phase is when we need to identify uncertainties, remove weak options, and select ideas that have the greatest potential to succeed. There are various techniques for doing this. In simple terms, we are balancing the amount of reward we expect from a potential concept against the risk of developing that concept and finding that it doesn't work. Using this type of approach, we can quickly categorise interventions into those that have high risk but low reward and so are probably not worth pursuing, those that are low risk and high reward and that we should definitely pursue, those that are low risk and low reward and that we should ignore, and those that are high reward and high risk and that might have potential but will need further exploration.

REFERENCES

Ajzen, I. (1991). The theory of planned behavior. *Organizational Behavior and Human Decision Processes, 50,* 179–211.

Herstatt, C., & Verworn, B. (2001). *The "fuzzy" front end of innovation.* Working Papers/Technologies-und Innovationsmanagment, No. 4, The Hamburg University of Technology. Retrieved from http://nbn-resolving.de/urn:nbn:de:gbv:830-opus-1637

Kahneman, D. (2012). *Thinking, fast and slow.* London: Penguin.

Khurana, A., & Rosenthal, S. R. (1998). Towards holistic "front ends" in new product development. *Journal of Product Innovation Management, 15*(1), 55–75.

Koen, P. A., Bertels, H. M. J., & Kleinschmidt, E. (2014). Managing the front end of innovation—Part 1: Results from a three-year study. *Research-Technology Management, 57*(2), 34–43.

Lewis, M. (2017). *The undoing project: A friendship that changed the world* (6th ed.). London: Penguin.

Val-Jauregi, E., & Justel, D. (2007). *Use of tools, methods and techniques during the fuzzy front end of innovation and their impact on innovation performance: A survey based exploratory study of companies in the Basque Country.* Presented at the International Conference on Engineering Design, ICED'07, Cite Des Science et De L'Industrie, Paris, France.

CHAPTER 6

The Importance of Multiple Perspectives

How to Make Behavioural Science Work in Multidisciplinary Teams

Abstract Behavioural science can be most effective when deployed as part of a multidisciplinary team. Furthermore, behavioural science is more likely than other functions to need to be part of a multidisciplinary team, as many functions touch on the way people interact with each other and with products and services. This chapter provides a brief overview of the academic literature about the benefits and challenges of working in multidisciplinary teams and describes a case study of how this works in practice. Rubinstein lays out guidelines for making multidisciplinary teamworking effective that include building trust, managing professional identities, coping with different communication styles, managing uncertainty, managing complexity, assessing quality, dealing with time pressures and availability, and the role of the leader.

Keywords Holistic innovation • Leadership • Multidisciplinary teamworking • Professional identity

At the beginning of a project about perfume, Guen, Gabe, and James were talking about smell. Guen, who has a background in pharmacology and is also a veterinary surgeon, was explaining to the team about how we smell a scent. *"Scent evaporates from the skin, enters the nose, and dissolves in the mucus layer. From there, it diffuses and binds to receptors which send a signal to your olfactory lobe, which is where the signal is processed in the brain."*

© The Author(s) 2018
H. Rubinstein, *Applying Behavioural Science to the Private Sector*,
https://doi.org/10.1007/978-3-030-01698-2_6

Gabe nodded. As a psychologist, he was interested in how this biological process affected how people perceived the perfume. *"It isn't just a chemical process,"* he commented. *"We perceive the scent in its totality across many of our senses—the intensity, the colour, the emotions it arouses, how warm it feels. Our experience is more than just sending smell signals to the brain."*

James, the product designer on the team, had a question. *"Why do you stop noticing a scent?"*

"That's called adaptation," explained Gabe. *"It means that your brain has decided to ignore the constant stimulus of the scent, so it can focus on other things."*

James looked thoughtful. *"How on earth does this help us to work out how to help women to choose the best perfume for them?"*

* * *

This sort of discussion is a common one at Innovia, especially in the 'understand stage' of a project. Consultants are trying to deconstruct the challenge and consider it from multiple perspectives. The individual members of the team all have different types of knowledge and varying degrees of experience of the problem they are engaging with.

The company fundamentally believes that working in multidisciplinary teams—a process that is referred to as holistic innovation—makes it possible to explore more options and create better answers than would be possible by deploying different specialisms sequentially. In this context, behavioural science is best used in combination with other disciplines. The behavioural scientists help the team to understand what matters to people, the designers help ensure ideas are attractive and easy to make and to use, and the technical specialists ensure that any new products or services are technically feasible. The result is consumer-testable, usable, technically feasible intervention directions and propositions.

But working in multidisciplinary teams is not easy. Over many years, Innovia has learned from what the literature says about multi-disciplinary working and integrated this into its own processes to enable people from very different backgrounds to work effectively together.

This chapter covers three aspects of multidisciplinary working: what the academic literature tells us about the benefits and challenges of working in multidisciplinary teams; the practical reality of working in multidisciplinary team (using Innovia as a case study); and guidelines for making multidisciplinary teams effective.

6.1   WHY WORK IN MULTIDISCIPLINARY TEAMS?

In certain areas, it is fairly common for multidisciplinary teams to be brought together to solve complex challenges. In innovation or new product development projects, members of the team may be drawn from marketing, R&D, operations, and commercial parts of the organisation. In health care, doctors, nurses, administrators, and specialist staff such as radiologists may be brought together to work out how to improve patient outcomes.

As a result, there is an extensive literature about the benefits and challenges of working in diverse teams. The basic assumption is that when members of the team have different professional competencies and a broader range of skills, they will generate more innovative, better quality, and more effective solutions (Alves, Marques, Saur, & Marques, 2007; Kearney, Gebert, & Voelpel, 2009; Vissers & Dankbaar, 2002). But is this always the case?

The evidence suggests that multidisciplinary working is effective in some but not all cases and that it is not without its difficulties (described below). Managing multidisciplinary teams is complex—it is not just about following a few simple rules. It may be necessary to try different approaches to see what works in a specific organisation or situation (Jackson, 1996).

6.1.1   What Are the Benefits?

People believe that multidisciplinary teams are good at addressing complex challenges for the following reasons.

* New knowledge is created (Edmondson & Nembhard, 2009)
* Knowledge is used more efficiently (Jackson, 1996)
* A wider range of perspectives is considered (Alves et al., 2007)
* More, and better creative solutions are developed (Jackson, 1996)
* Problem-solving is faster (Jackson, 1996)
* More efficient processes are developed (Jackson, 1996)

- Foresight of costs, benefits and side-effects is better (Cowan, 1986; Simon, 1987)
- Access to professional and social networks is wider (Vegt & Bunderson, 2005)
- There is interdepartmental transfer of information and ideas (Edmondson & Nembhard, 2009)
- Individual team members learn and improve performance—known as the 'assembly bonus effect' (Collins & Guetzkow, 1964)

This is a compelling list of advantages. Working in multidisciplinary teams can bridge gaps that result from disciplinary specialisation (Janssen & Goldsworthy, 1996) and helps to integrate different functions. Creativity can spring up at the boundaries of specialties and disciplines (Kanter & Summers, 1988, p. 176). The real benefits come from *integrating different perspectives* rather than from individual pieces of knowledge (Ratcheva, 2009).

Nevertheless, there are real challenges to making multidisciplinary teams effective. And the pay-off is not automatic.

6.1.2   What Are the Challenges?

When working in multidisciplinary teams, certain problems may be encountered. These problems will hinder the team's effectiveness.

- Poor communication—individuals have different terminologies and do not share a common language (Jackson, 1996; Love, Fong, & Irani, 2006). This can be even more difficult if professional identity is strong as some members are less likely to listen to or accept ideas from others (Fay, Borrill, Amir, Haward, & West, 2006)
- Lack of identification with other team members (Kearney et al., 2009), especially if they do not have shared values (Mental Health Commission, 2006) or some members are not as committed to the project as others (Fay et al., 2006)
- Personal and professional conflicts due to different emphases on what aspect of the problem is important. This can be exacerbated if there are also strong hierarchies in place where some individuals are accorded greater importance than others (Mental Health Commission, 2006; Strober, 2006)

- The failure to 'unlearn' traditional patterns of professional interaction (Fay et al., 2006)
- A lack of a commonly shared vision or goal (Majchrzak, More, & Faraj, 2011)
- A leader who is unable to moderate or shape informal norms (Fay et al., 2006)

These difficulties can be overcome in a number of ways. You need to choose the right people to participate in the team—people who have a high need for cognition (Petty, Briñol, Loersch, & McCaslin, 2009) (a tendency to engage in and enjoy thinking) actively enjoy finding ways to solve problems, welcome the opportunity to look for different options, want to share knowledge and actively contribute to discussions (Kearney et al., 2009). You need to be clear about the shared goal, and vision for the project and you need to actively foster a strong team identification (Vissers & Dankbaar, 2002).

Behavioural scientists can have an important role to play in overcoming these difficulties, not only because the behavioural perspective is often relevant to the task, but also because they will be more aware than most what is driving the behaviour of the team. They should be able to spot quickly why team members are feeling unmotivated, lack capability, or are unable to find the opportunity to exercise their expertise.

6.2   How to Work in Multidisciplinary Teams?

Alastair, Julian, Geraint, and Colin, the four original founders of Innovia Technology, started the company with a strong belief in the benefits of working in multidisciplinary teams—an approach that they described as 'holistic innovation'. All of them were physicists by training, but agreed that, to succeed, they needed to recruit outside of their discipline. They recruited product designers, biologists, medicinal chemists, vets, chemical engineers, strategists, biochemists, mathematicians, engineers, and material scientists. In 2014, the psychologists and neuroscientists arrived.

Over the years, the company has developed many ways to ensure that people from very different backgrounds are able to work effectively together. Colin, one of the founders, recalled that the company had to go through several levels of engagement in order to make holistic working a success.

"The first level was task-based—we had the designers working with the physicists. At this point, the physicists thought that the designers were just 'making it look nice' and so we sometimes dismissed their point of view on the function. The second level was request-based. We came to realise that designers brought a new perspective to the problem. For example, they knew better how people practically use a product. In my view, most people working in multidisciplinary teams get stuck at this level. The third level was transactional—we learned when and how to pass the parcel to different disciplines, we gave them something to do and they went off and did it. The fourth level is truly collaborative. This is where you get breakthroughs. Here there is real dialogue building and a holistic conversation. Things happen much more in parallel."

All the consultants at Innovia routinely work in 'holistic' teams. They vividly recall both good and bad experiences of adaptation.

Ben, head of design, recalled one particularly positive experience when he was leading a project for a novel eye-test demonstrator. He said it was one of the projects that he was most proud of but also one where he had been most scared. Here, he describes why this occurred.

"This was a technical problem. Patents were involved, and a paper was written for publication. There was uncertainty around whether the tests would work and indeed, half way through, nothing seemed to be working. I had to rely on the team and I had to admit that I (personally) didn't know what to do. This galvanised the team and we got through it together.

The team had already worked on an earlier part of the project and knew and trusted each other. The technical lead was very strong and importantly, was able to communicate in a language that others could understand, and the designers could use. This ability to translate into design language was critical. There was mutual respect, everyone understood what everyone else could do, and people had similar communication styles.

We didn't have much time to anticipate because deadlines were so tight, so we kept everyone on track by always thinking about the end point. We didn't know absolutely what the solution was going to be, but we kept a consistent narrative about what we were hoping to get to. It's all about managing expectations.

In this context I, as the leader, was the connector. I had to listen to all views—including the team and the client."

In contrast, Kora, a behavioural economist, reflected on a project that had successful results but where the team had difficulties working together because there were several new recruits not yet familiar with the holistic style.

"People's expectations were not well managed. Each person thought their own area was the most important. You need to be clear (in a big team) who is core and who is peripheral. When trust breaks down, it can be hard to tell someone from a different discipline what to do. Trust goes both ways—you have to trust the technical lead but still give guidance. You have to keep everyone focussed on the end goal."

Both of these accounts emphasise the importance of trust and respect between team members and this emerged as one of five major themes. These are:

1. Build trust and respect
2. Structure the process
3. Select people with the right characteristics
4. Keep sight of the end point
5. Appoint the right leader

6.2.1   Build Trust and Respect

As alluded to above, this is the foundation for multidisciplinary working. This includes but goes beyond individual respect: if team members do not respect others' functions or disciplines, then individual team members act in their own interests and not in the interests of the project. To a great extent, it is the team leader who is responsible for building trust between team members.

Trust is very important. If there is no trust, people will not volunteer ideas because they worry about seeming foolish. The more the team trust and respect each other, the easier it is to have open, wide-ranging discussions.

As Ben said, *"I always take time to get know people and keep everyone in the loop."*

6.2.2   Structure the Process

When you are working in a multidisciplinary team, there are many activities occurring simultaneously. Therefore, it is imperative that there is clear structure—a road map—so that people know where they are going. Innovia developed the Understand, Explore, Decide (UED) framework (referred to in Chap. 5) for this purpose. Without it, people lose direction and it is easy for someone to claim that their approach is more important than someone else's approach. Using a framework such as UED means that the team is tuned to multidisciplinary working right from the beginning.

Colin commented that, *"working in holistic teams is efficient because you can more easily recognise ideas that will be a waste of time, and those that will be good, right from the start."*

6.2.3   Select People with the Right Characteristics

Working in multidisciplinary teams is not for everyone. All the Innovians who were interviewed had clear views about the characteristics of those people who could work in this way. They needed to be able to communicate clearly, be comfortable with uncertainty, be able to admit if they don't know something, have high levels of intrinsic motivation, and a high need for cognition.

First and foremost was the ability to communicate about their area of specialisation in a way that non-specialists could understand.

Alex wondered whether, *"if you have teaching experience, does it make a difference? A lot of the scientists here have taught and know how to make an argument in a constructive way. This means that they can have a good-natured debate."*

Team members also have to have high levels of ambiguity tolerance (Budner, 2006) which means that they are comfortable in situations where there is a lot of change and the outcome is uncertain. They should be comfortable making tentative suggestions, even if they have not had time to think through all of the possible implications.

People also need to be humble and recognise that other people will have valuable skills that they don't. Individuals have to be happy to admit that they don't know everything (as Ben did in the example above) and not assume that their specialism is the most important.

People in these teams also need high levels of intrinsic motivation (Ryan & Deci, 2000) and a high need for cognition (Petty et al., 2009). People who are intrinsically motivated do things because they enjoy doing them rather than because they expect some external reward. Linked to this trait is a high need for cognition (Thompson, Chaiken, & Hazlewood, 1993). Individuals with a high need for cognition are curious, and have an increased appreciation of debate, idea evaluation, and problem solving. Innovia consultants are actively recruited for this trait.

Alex reflected that, *"people here are given space to explore and have to be open-minded. You can't know all the answers. Innovians are genuinely curious and are comfortable with not being right. Their specialisation is just an enabler. People do things because they have become interested (in them): sometimes the projects that seem dull (at the outset) turn out to be the most fascinating."*

6.2.4   Keep Sight of the End Point

Time and again, Innovia consultants mentioned that focussing on the end goal was a critical factor for success. This requires persistence, especially during periods when the project is not going to plan.

"The end point has to be made explicit," said Ben. *"Otherwise people don't know what they are aiming for and can go around in circles."*

6.2.5   Appoint the Right Leader

The leader has a key role to play in optimising team work. He or she is a coordinator and a guide.

Colin commented that, *"the functional skill set (of the leader) is not that important provided the team can communicate and the leader can understand and make a decision. However, the leader cannot lose the roadmap or sight of the objectives."*

As discussed above, the leader of the team cannot be expected to know everything and so has to depend on team members to perform their roles. The leader needs to protect the team and give them the space to do their best work. This means recognising the importance of professional identity.

Alex thought that, *"a team member might want to say something that is embryonic and be comfortable asking dumb questions. People might be really good in their field, but they have to be happy to take a risk. The leader can enable that."*

6.3   HOW TO PROMOTE MULTIDISCIPLINARY WORKING?

The consultants at Innovia recognise that it is necessary to work hard to make multidisciplinary teams work.

"You have to do it often. We are used to forming and reforming teams. It is normal here," said Ben.

Being able to work in a fluid way is important, because people go away to research on their own, and then come back together again. The more that teams work in this way, the more likely they are to succeed.

Colin thought that, *"once people have done this and succeeded, they become evangelical."* However, there are some preconditions to enabling success. One aspect is that most key meetings need to be face-to-face. Working remotely is not nearly so effective.

"We spend a lot of time working together in a room—the best way is face-to-face," explained Alex. *"Online chat is good but not a substitute. You need lots of ways to communicate. It is hard to make it work effectively if you work remotely."*

The Innovia consultants thought that it was important to avoid hierarchies. Hierarchies are problematic because team members lower down the hierarchy are less likely to contribute or speak out. To this end, Innovia has tried to keep the organisational structure as flat as possible.

So how to promote multidisciplinary working? Innovia created the Holistic Foundation Programme to train new consultants in this skill. The programme allows new consultants to sit in on projects that they are not necessarily working on day-to-day, and which involve disciplines other than their own. This exposes them to people with backgrounds very different from their own and helps them to understand how other functions work. This programme has become an important way to integrate new functions into multidisciplinary teams.

6.4   WHAT SHOULD LEADERS OF MULTIDISCIPLINARY TEAMS CONSIDER?

While many companies talk about the benefits of multidisciplinary teams, there is little practical guidance about how to get the most out of them. With the help of the behavioural scientists, Innovia has developed a toolkit of practical tips for project managers (Rose, 2016), and it shares these with consultants when they are learning to manage multidisciplinary teams.

The tips are grouped into the following categories: how to build trust, how to manage professional identities, how to cope with different communication styles, how to manage uncertainty, how to deal with complexity, how to assess quality of the output when this is outside your core capability, how to be a leader, and how to deal with time pressures and incomplete availability of team members.

6.4.1   How to Build Trust

Trust between team members is fundamental for multidisciplinary teams to work effectively. The team leader has an important role in helping to build trust: she should take time to understand the background and skills of team members to ensure that they are able to deliver their best work.

It is also the job of the team leader to keep the team 'in the loop', so that everyone knows what is happening, even when there are several work streams running concurrently. This is frequently the case on large, complex projects and the leader needs to give individual team members ownership, responsibility and accountability for what they do.

There are times during projects where a team member's time is in high demand and other times when they are not needed. Team members sometimes get despondent if they feel they are being side-lined, so it is important that the team leader is courteous and respectful of their time and motivations because commitment will be needed on some future project.

6.4.2   How to Manage Professional Identities

People's self-worth is linked to their professional identity and each team member has emotional ownership of their discipline. They want to demonstrate their expertise and can feel threatened if their advice is not listened to or accepted. The leader should try and put himself in the shoes of other team members and balance their needs with the needs of the project. Remember to recognise everyone's contribution and say, "thank you".

One of the benefits of working in a multidisciplinary team is the potential for cross-learning (getting new knowledge from outside your discipline). Cross-learning can be encouraged by asking people from one function or area of expertise to work outside their usual area. If all tasks are always allocated according to a specific area of expertise (for example, a biologist is only given work that relates to biology; a marketing executive is only asked to consider communications), the real benefits of multidisciplinary working will be lost.

Outputs from workstreams should not be isolated, but holistic. Share and build as much as possible. This has two advantages: one, it prevents individual team members from getting bogged down in individual tasks, and two, it allows problems to be identified collectively early on.

6.4.3   How to Cope with Different Communication Styles

It is highly likely that team members may communicate in different styles depending on their background. As psychologists, we may believe that the best way to design a product is to start with an understanding of the unmet needs of the consumers and define the challenge in human terms. In contrast, the physicists may feel that the best place to start is in working out how effective the technology is and describe the challenge as a series of mathematical equations. Both approaches provide helpful insights, but are incomplete on their own. The team leader should be aware of these disparities, and of her own professional style, in mediating between these points of view.

One tip from a project manager at Innovia was *"if you are unable to explain your professional perspective to a person from another discipline you may not fully understand it yourself."* This is a good check for any team leader or member of a multidisciplinary team. Terms that seem obvious and familiar in your professional area may be unknown by people in other professional areas. If you are aware of this it gives other team members permission to ask seemingly obvious questions such as the question James asked at the beginning of this chapter, *"why do you stop noticing scent?"*

6.4.4   How to Manage Uncertainty

In any new project, there is likely to be a large degree of uncertainty around how easy it will be to meet the agreed objectives. This is especially true for innovation or in areas where we are developing new knowledge or processes. This is to be expected, but there are things we can do to mitigate uncertainty at different stages of the project.

The tips here are as relevant for projects which are not multidisciplinary as for those where several disciplines are represented. However, it is even more important to manage uncertainty in multidisciplinary teams because if there is uncertainty, one discipline my attempt to dominate.

At the Start of the Project
It is important to be clear about the scope of what you intend to do: what is in scope and what isn't? Spending time on this early on helps keep the team on track and ensures that you do not waste time on activities that are outside the agreed scope. Being clear and explicit about the criteria for successful outcomes is also critical at this early stage.

Envision the endpoint at the start of the project: what does a successful endpoint look like and how does it fit into the bigger picture? This helps people stay focussed on what they aim to achieve even during the 'dip of despair': the point in a project where team members feel most despondent and uncertain (this is common and is discussed later).

Part of envisioning the endpoint is to predict the final deliverable as early as possible. Sketch out what the presentation story could look like— not the conclusion but an outline of the process, concept analysis and concepts. These are the hypotheses that you will test as you go through the process.

Throughout the Project
Understand the motivations, politics, and previous experience of team members and look out for signs that people are demotivated or need additional support. As mentioned earlier, behavioural scientists are likely to be alert to the signs of demotivation and may have strategies for how to deal with this problem.

The 'dip of despair' happens in most projects usually near the beginning or in the middle when the team is still trying to work out the key challenges. During these times, the team may be collecting and collating a lot of new information, which may not appear to make sense and there may not be many obvious solutions. The team leader should acknowledge that this is normal and take time to pause and reflect. The more time the team spend together thinking through the challenge, the more likely that the team will emerge from the dip!

One way to get though the 'dip of despair' is to test new ideas early on. For example, in an innovation project, start by focussing on uncovering the biggest uncertainties. If you can tackle the hardest problem early on, subsequent challenges will seem easier.

At the End of the Project
It is useful to have a team review of every multidisciplinary team project to identify what worked well and what could be improved. Appoint a reviewer who is neutral and not involved in the project to chair the meeting. During the review, give every team member a chance to say what they enjoyed, what they found difficult, and what they would recommend doing differently next time. During this process, the team leader should listen and refrain from disagreeing with other team members' points of view. The aim of the review is to learn and use the new information to improve team working in the future.

6.4.5   How to Deal with Complexity

Multidisciplinary teams are brought together for complex problems, which, by definition, are hard to solve. There are several activities that will help the team to navigate complexity.

First, *plan* the process. Use tools like Gantt charts to show how tasks fit together to achieve an efficient delivery with minimal stress. Plan by milestone rather than activity: in multidisciplinary projects the means to solve the challenge can be uncertain. The team leader needs to keep the team on track. Plan the communication of your output and make sure you reserve plenty of time and resource for this, as this stage is often overlooked.

Review the process at regular intervals. For example, have short weekly meetings to review the plan and keep the team focussed. This can be flexed as necessary: sometimes daily meetings may be needed.

Remember, don't lose sight of the *bigger picture*: show team members how their work fits in to the whole project and avoid piecemeal management as this is demotivating.

It is up to the team leader to *anticipate* problems and challenges: timing is critical when bringing teams together. If you do this too early, people haven't time to clarify their ideas but if you do this too late, you may lose the 'magic' when new ideas start to emerge.

Finally, remember to keep a *constant narrative*. In complex, multidisciplinary projects, team members can get lost. Recap in meetings and use process diagrams to remind team members (and clients) where the project is headed and where it has been.

6.4.6   How to Assess Quality of the Output When This Is Outside Your Core Capability

Delegating outside your own function or discipline can be unnerving. The team leader can't know everything, so plan the project with your team to get buy-in.

6.4.7   How to Be a Leader

Although the leader may not have knowledge of all the disciplines, she needs to be able to guide the team to the right place. There are distinct behaviours that leaders should follow to make the team more effective.

It is not unusual for debates and arguments to occur during a project. The team leader should *mediate* between different styles and opinions. Creative arguments are not always a bad thing, but the leader should not be afraid to challenge team members. It is during these discussions that new ideas emerge. *Listening* is an important skill for a team leader. The leader needs to be open to other points of view, be respectful of other people and not squash other people's ideas unthinkingly. Nevertheless, they should not be afraid to explain why an idea needs improving, or how it can be improved.

The team leader can also *connect* members of the team and make conversations happen. This is especially important for inexperienced team members who may not know when to talk to each other.

As discussed earlier, a major benefit of multidisciplinary working is that individual team members benefit from learning new things. The team leader can *encourage* team members to grow and develop, to experiment and even, in some cases, to fail. This builds an individual's confidence. Confident teams are the most productive.

We have already mentioned the 'dip of despair'. It is the role of the team leader to *be positive* in this time of doubt. Teams can think they have lost their way and feel disillusioned but the leader can be a positive force. Help the team to see that they haven't lost the way, they just have not yet found it. Don't expose the team to too much cynicism or negativity, particularly in difficult times during the project.

6.4.8   How to Deal with Time Pressures and Incomplete Availability of Team Members

During a project, individual team members will also be expected to work on other projects or in their main function. The team leader should *plan resources* carefully. The team leader needs to make it clear how much each team member is expected to spend on the project. And each team member needs to tell the leader if they do not have sufficient time to spend on the project. Pressures on time needs to be respected. Tight deadlines and multiple work commitments cause stress. The team leader can *acknowledge the high stress* that comes from tight deadlines and ensure that individual team member's time is protected wherever possible.

6.5   SUMMARY

More so than many functions, behavioural scientists need to work in multidisciplinary teams because many business activities concern the way people interact with each other, and with products and services.

While there are many benefits to working in this way, there are also many challenges to making multidisciplinary team-working effective. These include communication difficulties when specialists have different approaches and use different terminologies, team conflicts that can undermine professional identities, a lack of a shared vision or goal and leaders that fail to direct and motivate the team.

Time and patience are needed to ensure that multidisciplinary working is successful. It requires processes to be put in place to enable better working practices, attention to the characteristics of the team members, and clarity about the role and responsibility of the team leader.

Innovia has worked hard to make multidisciplinary working as smooth and effective as possible and has developed a toolkit of tips to build trust, manage professional identities, cope with different communication styles, manage uncertainty and complexity, assess quality of the output when this is outside their core capability, dealing with time pressures and being a leader.

When multidisciplinary teams are successful, team members not only report an enjoyable, satisfying, and memorable experience but also better and more effective solutions to the problems they are solving.

REFERENCES

Alves, J., Marques, M. J., Saur, I., & Marques, P. (2007). Creativity and innovation through multidisciplinary and multisectoral cooperation. *Creativity and Innovation Management, 16*(1), 27–34. https://doi.org/10.1111/j.1467-8691.2007.00417.x

Budner, S. (2006). Intolerance of ambiguity as a personality variable. *Journal of Personality, 30*(1), 29–50. https://doi.org/10.1111/j.1467-6494.1962.tb02303.x

Collins, B. E., & Guetzkow, H. (1964). *A social psychology of group processes for decision making*. New York: Wiley.

Cowan, D. A. (1986). Developing a process model of problem recognition. *Academy of Management Review, 11*(4), 763–776. https://doi.org/10.5465/AMR.1986.4283930

Edmondson, A. C., & Nembhard, I. M. (2009). Product development and learning in project teams: The challenges are the benefits*. *Journal of Product Innovation Management*, 26(2), 123–138. https://doi.org/10.1111/j.1540-5885.2009.00341.x

Fay, D., Borrill, C., Amir, Z., Haward, R., & West, M. A. (2006). Getting the most out of multidisciplinary teams: A multi-sample study of team innovation in health care. *Journal of Occupational and Organizational Psychology*, 79(4), 553–567. https://doi.org/10.1348/096317905X72128

Jackson, S. E. (1996). The consequences of diversity in multidisciplinary work teams. In *Handbook of work group psychology* (pp. 53–75). Chichester, UK: John Wiley & Sons, Ltd.

Janssen, W., & Goldsworthy, P. (1996). Multidisciplinary research for natural resource management: Conceptual and practical implications. *Agricultural Systems*, 51(3), 259–279. https://doi.org/10.1016/0308-521X(95)00046-8

Kanter, R. M., & Summers, D. (1988). When a thousand flowers bloom: Social, structural and collective conditions for innovation in organizations. In *Research in organizational behavior* (Vol. 10). Greenwich, CT: Elsevier.

Kearney, E., Gebert, D., & Voelpel, S. C. (2009). When and how diversity benefits teams: The importance of team members' need for cognition. *Academy of Management Journal*, 52(3), 581–598. https://doi.org/10.5465/AMJ.2009.41331431

Love, P., Fong, P., & Irani, Z. (2006). *Management of knowledge in project environments*. London: Routledge.

Majchrzak, A., More, P. H. B., & Faraj, S. (2011). Transcending knowledge differences in cross-functional teams. *Organization Science*, 23(4), 951–970. https://doi.org/10.1287/orsc.1110.0677

Mental Health Commission. (2006). *Multi-disciplinary team working: From theory to practice*. Dublin: Coimisiún Meabhair-Shláinte, Dublin. Retrieved from http://www.mhcirl.ie/File/discusspapmultiteam.pdf

Petty, R. E., Briñol, P., Loersch, C., & McCaslin, M. J. (2009). The need for cognition. In *Handbook of individiual differences in social behaviour* (pp. 318–329). New York: Guilford Press.

Ratcheva, V. (2009). Integrating diverse knowledge through boundary spanning processes—The case of multidisciplinary project teams. *International Journal of Project Management*, 27(3), 206–215. https://doi.org/10.1016/j.ijproman.2008.02.008

Rose, B. (2016). *Managing multidisciplinary teams effectively: Tips for project managers*. Innovia Technology.

Ryan, R. M., & Deci, E. L. (2000). Self-determination theory and the facilitation of intrinsic motivation, social development, and well-being. *The American Psychologist*, 55(1), 68–78.

Simon, H. A. (1987). Making management decisions: The role of intuition and emotion. *Academy of Management Executive, 1*(1), 57–64.

Strober, M. H. (2006). Habits of the mind: Challenges for multidisciplinary engagement. *Social Epistemology, 20*(3–4), 315–331. https://doi.org/10.1080/02691720600847324

Thompson, E. P., Chaiken, S., & Hazlewood, J. D. (1993). Need for cognition and desire for control as moderators of extrinsic reward effects: A person x situation approach to the study of intrinsic motivation. *Journal of Personality and Social Psychology, 64*(6), 987–999.

Vegt, G. S. V. D., & Bunderson, J. S. (2005). Learning and performance in multidisciplinary teams: The importance of collective team identification. *Academy of Management Journal, 48*(3), 532–547. https://doi.org/10.5465/AMJ.2005.17407918

Vissers, G., & Dankbaar, B. (2002). Creativity in multidisciplinary new product development teams. *Creativity and Innovation Management, 11*(1), 31–42. https://doi.org/10.1111/1467-8691.00234

A Case Study of Using Behavioural Science in Practice

How Southwest Airlines Used It to Improve the Boarding Experience

Abstract This is a detailed case study about how behavioural science was applied to improve the boarding experience at the gate that satisfied the needs of passengers, employees, and the airline operator, Southwest Airlines. The case study shows how the principles for applying behavioural science described in earlier chapters were used to solve the challenge. In this chapter, Rubinstein outlines the activities that enabled the development of a behavioural model of passenger behaviour, and how a five-step approach to intervention design was applied. It ends by showing some of the solutions that were devised and describes the results of a testing programme in a real-life situation in an airport in the USA.

Keywords Behavioural diagnosis • Intervention design • Team building • Intervention testing

In February 2015, the innovation team from Southwest Airlines (Southwest) and a small team from Innovia Technology were sitting in a meeting room at their Love Field offices in Dallas, Texas, discussing an issue that the Southwest team had been thinking about for some time.

© The Author(s) 2018
H. Rubinstein, *Applying Behavioural Science to the Private Sector*,
https://doi.org/10.1007/978-3-030-01698-2_7

"The thing is," said Heather, who was Senior Director of Innovation at the airline. *"The boarding process works fine, but it could be improved. We know that waiting to board the plane is a pain point for our customers and we want to make that better. At the same time, we want to make it faster so that we can stick to our schedules even more. And whatever changes we make, they must reflect our values. Everyone has the right to the same good level of service and we are 'high touch'—we will never use technology just for the sake of it."*

The Innovia team were already buzzing with questions.

"What do we know about the psychology of queuing and waiting around? What bothers people?" I asked.

Arron was concerned about logistics at the airport. *"Who owns the boarding gate—the airport or the airline?"*

Glenn was thinking about all the activities that occur before you even get to the gate. *"Everything that happens beforehand also contributes to the experience."*

And Ben was thinking about the confusing airport signage. *"I'm quite sure we can do much better,"* he said.

Over the next few hours, the team thrashed out the scope of the project. The journey to improve the experience at the boarding gate had begun.

*   *   *

Southwest Airlines was founded in 1967 in San Antonio, Texas by Herb Kelleher and Rollin King. Right from the start, its approach was groundbreaking—it has been the inspiration for most of the low-cost airlines around the world. Today, it employs over 57,000 people and, in the peak season, operates more than 4000 flights a day. The airline industry is highly cyclical and not known for sustaining profitability—compared with most, Southwest has been a beacon of success. Part of the reason for this is its reputation for efficiency combined with friendliness and reliability. Passengers are treated with respect and there is a policy of transparency and openness. These values have contributed to Southwest becoming one of the most loved, most flown, and most profitable airlines.

In contrast with many other airlines, Southwest also has a reputation for being innovative. This new project was just another example of its progressive mindset—it is not afraid to try new things to stay ahead of the competition. Heather had contacted Innovia because of its reputation for tackling complex innovation problems in a rigorous and creative way.

What follows is the story of how Innovia worked with Southwest to transform the experience of boarding at the gate and to make boarding faster.

7.1   How the Team Was Selected

The first thing that Innovia had to do was to identify the right team to put on to the project. It was clear from the beginning that this challenge needed multidisciplinary perspectives to ensure that the eventual solutions satisfied the needs of not only the passengers but also the employees, the airports, and the airline.

I was brought in as a behavioural scientist with a background in social psychology. My role was to explore the perspective of the passenger and, in particular, to understand the psychology of travelling and how people interact with each other and with employees. I was also deputed as team leader to manage the project.

As a transport designer, Glenn brought an understanding of the complex nature of mass transport systems and how different elements needed to work together.

Arron's skills in engineering were needed to understand the complex systems, logistics, and cost models.

The other member of the team was Ben, a product designer by training who led the design function at Innovia. Ben was especially good at communicating and simplifying complex ideas to help people understand them easily.

These four were the core members of the team for the next nine months. As needed, others were brought in to help with specific activities.

My first task was to build trust within the team and create an environment where everyone could work together. I set up a project room—rather unimaginatively called P6—where the team could work. The idea was to find a 'safe' space where people could think, toss ideas around, and be creative. P6 was ideal. One side was a window looking out on to the peaceful River Cam and on the other three walls were whiteboards where ideas could be scribbled and pinned up during the project.

Although the team members worked in different parts of the building, this space became the central meeting point for the duration of the project.

Early meetings were focussed on allowing team members to share ideas about how they could approach the challenge and finding out how everybody could best contribute. At this early stage, I was content for individual players to come up with different approaches in a seemingly unstructured way because this meant that everyone could begin to learn each other's language. This turned out to be time well spent because not everyone had worked together before. The first few discussions allowed people to get to know each other and to recognise what each person brought to the project.

7.2   How the Team Identified the Right Problem to Solve

Early discussions centred on what problem the team was really trying to solve. The objective, as described by Heather, was to make the boarding experience better and faster. But what does "better" mean in this context? What aspects of the experience should change and what has to stay the same?

There was one fundamental constraint that had to be acknowledged: Southwest would not pre-allocate seats to make boarding faster. For many years, Southwest passengers have not been able to book a seat in advance, although passengers can get priority boarding. For example, they can buy an early-bird ticket, so they can board before other passengers, or if they are frequent flyers they may be a member of the Rapid Rewards scheme and get A-list boarding.

The reason for this is, as Heather stated, *"is because we want everyone to get the same high-quality level of service. Everyone should be treated in the same way."*

Armed with this information, the team devised a programme of activities to look at the boarding experience from multiple perspectives—the 'Understand' phase. It consisted of five separate activities.

1. A systematic analysis of the total passenger experience journey from booking to disembarkation: this was to understand 'pain' and 'pleasure points' and to find out what was driving behaviour
2. A review of the psychology of travelling and queuing to see what coping strategies people use
3. A look at the future of air travel and the anticipated changes to airports in the next few years to ensure that ideas would be robust to change

4. Investigation of analogous situations where people have to queue to see what could be learned from others who have to manage similar challenges
5. A review of key trends related to transport and the technical enablers that might be available to see whether there were novel solutions that could be applied

Activities 1 and 2 became the responsibility of the behavioural scientists; activities 3 and 4 were taken on by the design and logistics experts; and activity 5 came under transport specialist Glenn's remit.

After several weeks of investigation, and many more meetings to discuss their findings the team got back together again to refine the objective and agree where to focus.

"There are going to be loads more passengers in the future," Ben said. *"By the mid 2030s, the number of passengers going through airports will have doubled."*

Arron nodded. *"Sure, it will be much busier, but by then many processes will be automated, so getting through the airport itself could be quicker. On the other hand, that could lead to people spending even more time at the boarding gate."*

"That will just make the boarding process worse," I responded. *"Our analysis shows that people may get anxious, stressed and irritated when they are waiting, especially if they are uncertain about what to do next, or if they are in an unfamiliar environment."*

"Others have worked out how to deal with that problem," said Glenn. *"Disney have long ago worked out to manage people's expectations when they wait in line for long periods to get on a ride."*

After much discussion, the team finally agreed on the real challenges. These were to:

- *Relieve anxiety* throughout the journey and at the gate
- Improve the *physical environment* at the gate, to make boarding easier and more intuitive
- *Change the tasks and activities* at the boarding gate to make waiting less stressful and boring

7.3   How the Team Approached the Problem

To solve the problem, the Innovia team agreed to follow the five-step approach described in Chap. 4. That is, they:

1. Understood the problem in context
2. Defined the intervention space
3. Designed the interventions
4. Selected the interventions
5. Evaluated the interventions

7.3.1   Understood the Problem in Context

The first task was to define the behaviours that needed to be influenced. Over a period of weeks, the behavioural scientists observed passengers going through airports and waiting at the boarding gate. They asked leisure and business passengers to describe what they were doing, thinking, and feeling throughout the journey from booking the flight to getting off the plane. They reviewed existing data provided by Southwest and reviewed papers on the psychology of queuing and how people perceived the passing of time.

7.3.2   Defined the Intervention Space

Together, these activities enabled Innovia to build up an overview of the passenger journey from start to finish, identifying pain and pleasure points, and creating a model of the passenger experience. The analysis confirmed that the boarding gate was a major pain point for both leisure and business travellers. Furthermore, Southwest had more power to influence the boarding gate experience compared with other pain points like the security area.

For passengers, arriving at the gate is a point where anticipation and anxiety merge. Having got through check-in, worked their way through security and navigated through the airport, they have arrived at their point of departure at last. They are keen to get going but know they have to queue.

Some have already started queuing whilst others are working out queuing tactics. Some don't understand the boarding process and are confused, other are bored and frustrated. They try to distract themselves by reading or looking at their phones but are on high alert so as not to miss an announcement that might apply to them. They watch the screens obsessively to check for any hint of delay or change. They eye up other passengers surreptitiously for signals that the final queue is starting to form and are unsure whether or not to approach staff at the gate who seem to be busy. Frequent flyers are often irritated by those who rarely fly because they don't know where to go or don't have their documentation with them, holding up the queue.

The team systematically deconstructed all these activities at the gate to work out what and where to influence. The areas of influence are summarised in Fig. 7.1. The team used this framework for generating ideas to improve the experience of boarding at the gate.

7.3.3   Designed Interventions

This detailed analysis and model of behaviours at the gate was vital to help the team to generate solutions that would speed up and improve the experience.

I started the conversation. *"The atmosphere and the physical environment are really important. Crowding makes people stressed, and ambience affects people's mood. If we can alter the physical environment, we can help to reduce stress and make people feel calmer."*

Ben agreed. *"Designing an intuitive space can help to reduce uncertainty. When people feel uncertain, they feel frustrated and anxious, and when people feel anxious, time seems to drag on and on."*

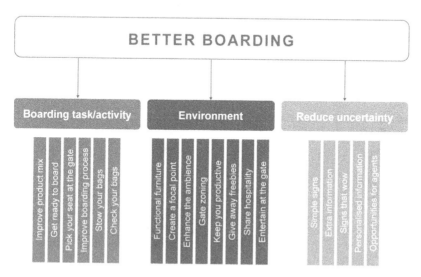

Fig. 7.1   Areas to influence at the boarding gate

"I agree," I responded. *"Unexplained waits always seem longer and lack of knowledge just increases confusion and stress. We can reduce anxiety by providing information about why people are waiting."*

"Information is really important," Arron confirmed. *"Getting information to people at exactly the right moment helps to reduce uncertainty. And if we can also encourage positive interactions with staff at the gate, people are more likely to know what is going on."*

"People really want to get going at this point," Glenn commented. *"They hate wasting time but if we can break up the tasks it will seem faster. When people are occupied, they are not thinking about time passing. We can provide distractions to alter their perceptions of time spent waiting."*

The Innovia team generated many concepts to improve the boarding experience. These had to reduce the time taken to board the plane and be aligned with the Southwest brand values of friendliness, efficiency, and transparency. Additionally, the concepts had to be realistic for the staff, and improve their job satisfaction. The team explored solutions that were simple and low-tech as well as those that made greater use of technology and were keen to ensure a balance of concepts that could be implemented in the short-term as well as those that required longer term development. Examples of concepts that provide information to relieve anxiety are shown in Fig. 7.2. The low-tech solution provides information about

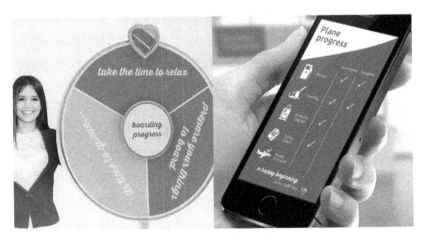

Fig. 7.2 Examples of high- and low-tech solutions to relieve anxiety at the boarding gate. Source: Innovia Technology

when to queue; the high-tech solution is a smart phone app that provides information about how the plane is being prepared while passengers wait at the gate.

7.3.4   Prioritised and Selected Interventions

At a working session with Southwest in Dallas, these ideas were reviewed and categorised according to impact—their ability to make the experience faster and more pleasant—and implementability—the ease with which they could be put in place. At the end of a long day, eleven concepts were considered worth pursuing (see Fig. 7.3).

"*I think we need to put these into tests,*" Heather asserted. "*Otherwise, we won't know what works and what doesn't, and we won't be able to validate the thinking that led us to them.*"

Erin, another member of the Southwest team, agreed. "*We need to develop them and place them at a test site. First, we need to know if passengers have a better experience than today and second, we need to know if it makes the process of boarding faster.*"

Fig. 7.3 Schematic of concepts tested at St Louis Airport. Source: Innovia Technology

7.3.5   Evaluated the Interventions

The Innovia team refined the concepts and sent them back to Southwest for the acid test. Would they work at a real boarding gate, with real passengers?

The ideas were tested at St Louis Airport for 12 weeks. With our interventions, boarding time was reduced on average by four minutes. This is very significant when the normal turnaround time for a plane from landing to embarking is 25 minutes. Furthermore, the changes reflected well on the airline: passengers felt that *"Southwest Airlines is a progressive, modern, and innovative, and it really cares about its customers"*.

7.4   SUMMARY

- The challenge of improving the boarding experience at the gate benefited from using a multidisciplinary team who could tackle the issue from diverse perspectives
- The role of behavioural science was to ensure that the concepts generated were grounded in an understanding of passenger psychology and behaviour. This helped ensure that the solutions would not only be effective at reducing the boarding times but also be acceptable to passengers and employees
- The concepts covered a wide spectrum of options, including changes that could be made immediately and changes that needed longer term development
- The process was systematic and rigorous. The team:

    - understood the problem in context to diagnose critical influences on behaviour
    - defined the intervention space (the physical environment, the tasks, and uncertainty)
    - designed interventions to address the challenge
    - selected (prioritised) the concepts, and
    - evaluated them in an experimental test

CHAPTER 8

The Ethical Risks of Behavioural Science

How to Avoid Its Misuse

Abstract Behavioural science is a powerful tool that can influence behaviour and for this reason there should be guidelines to ensure that it is used ethically. In this chapter, Rubinstein outlines the debate about the ethics of nudging in the public sector where, despite being used to promote good behaviour, it has been accused of 'soft paternalism' and the removal of free choice. She argues that although people are suspicious of its use in the private sector, there is a precedent for self-regulation and good use. Behavioural science in the private sector does not have to be deceitful, covert or manipulative. Furthermore, consumers have a different relationship with private companies than they have with policy makers. To avoid potential misuse, she suggests five guidelines to help practitioners make better decisions.

Keywords Behavioural research • Ethical guidelines • Soft paternalism

"I honestly don't know what to do about this," said Shreyas, as he began the meeting that he'd hastily organised. His team was working on a project about getting people to reduce their sugar intake and they were about to run an experiment in a real-life situation.

"What's the problem?" asked Hannah, the designer working alongside the behavioural scientists and public-health experts.

© The Author(s) 2018
H. Rubinstein, *Applying Behavioural Science to the Private Sector*,
https://Doi.org/10.1007/978-3-030-01698-2_8

117

"I've just received an email from our client. He wants to add another intervention to our tests in the restaurant. But I think he wants us to restrict people's access to some foods," replied Shreyas.

"What's the problem? It sounds like a good 'nudge' idea," said Hannah.

But Fiona looked worried. As the psychologist on the team, she knew that sometimes there are unintended consequences resulting from even the best of intentions. *"I can see how this could be a problem,"* she said. *"It's not fair to restrict options for those people who are unaffected."*

"I think we need to regroup," Shreyas said. *"We have an ethics review process for just this sort of issue. We need to be aware of not only the intended, but also the unintended, consequences of what we do."*

* * *

This sort of issue often arises when we are designing behaviour change programmes because changing behaviour is often a dialogue between the mental models of different people. Mental models are assumptions, generalisations, theories, beliefs, and images that we hold about ourselves, others, institutions, and phenomena. These models influence how we behave. Almost all behaviour change involves bringing people together who have different mental models. One person's mental model may mean that they do not perceive the same threats or risks of an action. For this reason, we need a framework to be able to debate these differences. Behavioural science is a powerful tool that can change people's behaviour, and we need some guidelines to ensure we use it wisely.

8.1   What Do We Need to Consider When Using Behavioural Science?

As we've shown, behavioural science can be used to change people's behaviour for their benefit. Seemingly trivial changes to the way we convey information, the way we arrange choices, or how we use 'default' choices[1] can affect how people behave. There has been a lively debate in

---

[1] *Default options* are options selected automatically unless an alternative is specified, and setting defaults is an effective tool in choice architecture when there is inertia or uncertainty in decision making.

the public sector about the ethics of using 'nudges.' These arguments could be relevant for the private sector. What do we need to be aware of when we apply behavioural science? Let's look at how behavioural science can be used badly and used well.

8.1.1   What Is Misuse?

Most people have become familiar with behavioural science through 'nudge theory' (described in more detail in Chap. 1). This is where the criticism about ethics has been most prevalent. Critics of nudging say that it is deceitful and manipulative. They are concerned that nudging relies on exploiting a variety of human biases by manipulating the environment, and taking advantage of a pattern of behaviour without a person's consent (Moles, 2015).

When we manipulate a person's choice, even if it is for their own good, we are treating them like a child, reducing their autonomy by altering their free will to make a decision (Ashcroft, 2013; Saghai, 2013). Nudging has been described as 'soft paternalism',[2] as it does not respect people's choices. Furthermore, nudges are not transparent. Consumers are concerned about hidden consent (the sort of consent where users are charged exorbitant rates if they forget to specify what they want). Regulators were aware of this when creating the General Data Protection Regulation (GDPR) (EU GDPR Information Portal, n.d.), a legal framework that sets guidelines for the collection and processing of personal information of individuals within the European Union. It stipulates that individuals "have the right not to be subject to a decision" if it is automatic and it produces a significant effect on a person.

When someone manipulates a person's choice, that 'nudger' may get it wrong as they may have biases of their own (Glaeser, 2005). They may want to push ahead with a programme because they feel it is for the good of the person being nudged and may become annoyed when the people being nudged disagree with them.

---

[2] *Paternalism* refers to acting for the good of another person against their will or without their consent. Hard paternalism occurs when you prevent someone from taking a harmful action, such as if you banned people from swimming in a dangerous place. Soft paternalism occurs when you coax someone to prevent them from taking a harmful action, such as if you put up signs on the beach telling people not to swim at specific times.

Nudgers may also be too quick to portray people's preferences as irrational when their decisions are actually based on sound, or at least reasonable, grounds (Glaeser, 2005). People may be predictable in their irrationality but they are not stupid. They may know that they need to exert self-control to select the healthy salad over the chips or pasta but deliberately choose not to, especially if they are not currently on a diet!

8.1.2   What Is Good Use?

Proponents of 'nudging' argue that, by definition, a nudge alters the choice architecture without coercing people, so respect for choice is maintained (Sunstein, 2015a).

Moreover, many nudges are intended to improve people's welfare and in such cases it would be ethically wrong *not* to nudge them (Sunstein, 2015b). In fact, nudges can promote autonomy: making decisions becomes easier, so people are freed up to focus on more important concerns. The 'paradox of choice' describes the fact that just because some choice is good, it does not mean that more choice is necessarily better. Too much choice can be overwhelming and can lead to poor decision-making. Using nudges helps people to make more rational and better decisions (Schwartz, 2004).

Additionally, nudges do not have to be covert or manipulative. Nudges can be transparent and still be effective when the reasons behind them are explained (Bruns, Kantorowicz-Reznichenko, Klement, Jonsson, & Rahali, 2016).

Although the nudgers may be biased, proponents of nudging say that their methods are fair provided that they are acting with the best intentions, base their actions on the available evidence, and ask people for consent to being nudged (Sunstein, 2016).

8.2   How Does This Affect the Private Sector?

This debate is by no means resolved. However, practitioners of nudging in the private sector can learn from the discussion. While some businesses will not be as ethical as we would wish, it is not in the interest of most companies to be dishonest and deceitful with their customers because of the potential reputational damage.

Persuasion using behavioural science does not have to be deceitful or manipulative. Nudges do not have to be covert and consent does not have to be hidden. We can help people to make better decisions by making the choice more intuitive. We can use science and evidence to make better choices, and to design products and services that actually satisfy consumer needs.

There are some additional factors to be taken into consideration. Consumers have a different relationship with private companies than they have with politicians and policy makers. They expect that companies will want to make a profit. They expect that companies will try to sell to them. There is an implicit contract between the consumer and the brand owner. *"We know what you are up to, but we will listen to what you have to say. We think this is OK as long as you inform and entertain us, and you don't lie."*

Frequent exposure to marketing and advertising means that people are 'savvy consumers': they know how to decode the messages. People expect a level of 'game playing' from companies that they would not tolerate from a 'nanny-state' government. In a 2015 Nielsen survey, 63% of respondents claimed to trust adverts in newspapers and 58% trusted adverts in magazines (Global Trust in Advertising—Neilsen, 2015). In contrast, only 21% trusted politicians (Ipsos MORI Poll, Politicians are still trusted less than estate agents, journalists and bankers, 2013).

In summary, the use of behavioural science does not have to be deceitful, covert, or manipulative. Businesses can use behavioural science for good and may have more license to use behavioural science than the public sector, provided they are not dishonest. There are those that believe that businesses will always tend towards unethical behaviour if left unchecked, but it is a counsel of despair to assume that all businesses are dishonest or that there is little we can do to ensure that we use behavioural science in an ethical manner. We can, and must, do better.

8.3   What Can We Learn from History?

Before we begin to outline what sort of guidelines might be developed, it is worth pausing to note that this is not the first time that a psychological approach from the private sector has been criticised. In the mid-twentieth century, the case of the Hidden Persuaders raised similar ethical questions.

In 1957, a journalist called Vance Packard published a book called The Hidden Persuaders (Packard, 1957). Packard argued that the advertising industry was using unscrupulous techniques to persuade unsuspecting consumers to buy products they didn't need. His major criticism was in the use of 'motivational research'. Motivational research, like nudging, had its foundations in psychology. The basic premise was that consumers could not be trusted to behave rationally, did not always know what they wanted, and did not always tell the truth to market researchers. Motivational-research techniques aimed to dig deeper into understanding consumer preferences by investigating their pre-conscious and subconscious motivations. The tools and techniques of the motivational researchers included in-depth interviews, projective tests, the use of hidden symbols to tap into our innermost desires and supposedly, subliminal advertising, which tapped into the unconscious mind.

Packard described an experiment that showed that moviegoers could be induced to buy more Coca Cola if they were repeatedly shown ads for Coca Cola for 0.0003 seconds. Despite the facts that the experiment could not be replicated, that there was no other evidence that subliminal advertising worked, and that the advertising industry was not actually using subliminal advertising, there was widespread moral outrage at the idea of such manipulation. The book became a bestseller.

It is interesting to learn how society reacted when this book was published, as there are parallels with the debate around nudging today.

First, there was governmental overreaction. Despite the lack of evidence for the effectiveness of subliminal communication, the Federal Trade Commission and the Federal Communications Commission issued policy statements prohibiting the use of this advertising technique.

Second, there was a concerted effort to produce some guidelines. The advertising and research community responded to the criticisms made by Packard and reviewed the methodologies they used. There was a move to ensure that advertising claims were *'legal, decent, honest, and truthful'* (Advertising Standards Authority & Committee of Advertising Practice, 2011). In 1961, the UK Advertising Standards Authority was set up to ensure that advertising worked for *'the benefit of consumers, business and society'*. In the US, the Federal Trade Commission stated that *'under the law, claims in advertisements must be truthful, cannot be deceptive or unfair, and must be evidence based'*.

As we have already noted, people did not reject advertisements. Trust in advertising still remains surprisingly high. There are several reasons for this. The guidelines acted to reassure people, representatives from across the industry came together to enforce the guidelines that regulate their activities, and consumers were given a channel through which they could directly express their concerns to the enforcers. This system works well. In 2017, the Advertising Standards Authority resolved 27,138 complaints from the public and as a result 19,398 ads were either withdrawn or amended.

In this instance, a voluntary code backed by adjacent legislation has yielded an approach that is acceptable to all parties.

8.4   HOW CAN WE USE BEHAVIOURAL SCIENCE ETHICALLY?

It's clear that, to take an ethical approach to behavioural science, we need to be aware of both the advantages and the disadvantages of this technique. We need to avoid the (unfounded) publicity storm surrounding the Hidden Persuaders. We can navigate the ethical pitfalls by setting out some guidelines for appropriate, ethical use of behavioural science in the private sector.

At present, no country forbids companies or policymakers from using biases, nor is there any overt form of 'behavioural-science regulation'. There is some evidence that policy makers are aware of behavioural-science intentions when they make laws to protect consumers. In one example, the European Commission managed to prevent Google from bundling products based on the default design of the content, and in another, there has been some legislation about privacy contained in the General Data Protection Regulation (EU GDPR Information Portal, n.d.). This regulation specifies that consent must be voluntary, come from a request, and be easy to withdraw from. It must also clearly explain whether it is necessary, or only preferable, to give consent for the company to access or process your data. Legislators, at least in Europe, are already considering how to prevent misuse of behavioural science principles.

There are cultural and philosophical differences between the Americans and the Europeans. In the US, there is a cultural tenet that people should be completely free to make their own choices, even if the outcome is poor. Thus, protecting consumers from corporations is seen as highly paternalistic: if people behave differently because of their biases, it is a simple mistake. The state should not prevent people from making their own mistakes (Copetinas, 2016). In contrast, the Europeans believe that it is the role of the state to protect consumers from companies that encourage poor choices. This means that US legislation, if it happens, is likely to be significantly slower than regulation in European countries.

On November 15, 2016, I proposed tentative guidelines for using behavioural science in a LinkedIn blog post (Rubinstein, 2016) and asked for feedback from practitioners. These broad guidelines suggested that limiting choice or making it difficult for people to choose otherwise are unethical, that behavioural interventions built on untruths are unacceptable, and that behaviourally based interventions should be scrutinised for unintended, as well as for intended, consequences.

The blog received many responses, but opinion was divided. Some people felt that this was a doomed endeavour. One response stated, *"Nudging is deceit. It would not pass scientific merit. It's that simple. Find a different way where you don't have to play mind games with your participants."*

Another felt that the use of nudges in the private sector was not appropriate. *"To me, this implies that nudges are a public-policy tool, not a tool for private-sector marketing. As others have commented here, private marketers use people's biases and limited information to sell things and make profits, not to promote the greater good."*

The vast majority of responses, however, were supportive. Several people commented that this is an important issue and although difficult, *"it is laudable to adopt specific ethical rules."*

Some commented that, given the increase in the number of behavioural architects operating in the private sector, the time is right to instigate a code for practitioners. Several suggested that a code would help marketers to take personal responsibility and *"to examine that line in every case to determine whether it has been crossed. Taking that time serves the marketer, the company, and its customers well for the long term."*

Respondents had different concerns and priorities: the main themes were concerns about lack of transparency, inadequate sharing of information and the errors that can be made by nudgers if they, themselves, are biased. There was also a recognition that any guidelines that are developed need to go beyond 'nudging' to include the broader use of behavioural science interventions. To this end, it was suggested that practitioners could take an online assessment to be accredited and included in a register of names of individuals who comply with a professional code of ethics.

It is early days for the application of such a young science and we are some way off creating a register or from having a professional code. In the spirit of this discussion, as a starting point, I suggested the following guidelines:

1. Behavioural interventions built on untruths are unacceptable
2. Nudges that make it difficult for people to choose otherwise are unethical: people must have the freedom to choose differently
3. Behavioural interventions should be scrutinised for unintended, as well as intended, consequences
4. Consent should not be hidden: interventions should be transparent wherever possible
5. Practitioners should be comfortable to defend their approach, methods and motives in public

8.5   Summary

Behavioural science is a powerful new tool. It has the potential to help people make better choices and seems to be an effective way to change behaviour without coercion.

Used well, behavioural science in the private sector does not have to be deceitful, covert or manipulative. Businesses can and should use behavioural science for the public good. Furthermore, consumers have a different relationship with private companies than they have with politicians and policy makers.

But it also has the potential to be misused: in practice these theoretical approaches have real world consequences. It is possible to change behaviours, sometimes without people being aware of it and there can be unintended consequences.

It is a grey area and there will always be debate. As a result, we need ethical guidelines because it is possible to cause harm to individuals and social groups. The five recommendations suggested here are just the starting point.

References

Advertising Standards Authority, & Committee of Advertising Practice. (2011). *Celebrating 50 years: Legal, decent, honest and truthful* (Annual Report). London.

Ashcroft, R. E. (2013). Doing good by stealth: Comments on 'Salvaging the concept of nudge'. *Journal of Medical Ethics, 39*(8), 494–494. https://doi.org/10.1136/medethics-2012-101109

Bruns, H., Kantorowicz-Reznichenko, E., Klement, K., Jonsson, M. L., & Rahali, B. (2016). *Can nudges be transparent and yet effective?* (SSRN Scholarly Paper

No. ID 2816227). Rochester, NY: Social Science Research Network. Retrieved from https://papers.ssrn.com/abstract=2816227

Copetinas, V. (2016). Ethics of nudging. Personal correspondence.

EU GDPR Information Portal. (n.d.). Retrieved July 26, 2018, from http://eugdpr.org/eugdpr.org-1.html

Glaeser, E. L. (2005). *Paternalism and psychology*. Working Paper 11789, National Bureau of Economic Research, Cambridge, MA.

Global Trust in Advertising. (2015). Retrieved September 27, 2016, from http://www.nielsen.com/eu/en/insights/reports/2015/global-trust-in-advertising-2015.html

Ipsos MORI|Poll|Politicians are still trusted less than estate agents, journalists and bankers. (2013). Retrieved September 27, 2016, from https://www.ipsos-mori.com/researchpublications/researcharchive/3685/Politicians-are-still-trusted-less-than-estate-agents-journalists-and-bankers.aspx

Moles, A. (2015). Nudging for liberals. *Social Theory and Practice, 41*(4), 644–667. https://doi.org/10.5840/soctheorpract201541435

Packard, V. (1957). *The hidden persuaders*. New York: D. McKay Co.

Rubinstein, H. (2016). *Behavioural science in the private sector*. Innovia Technology. Retrieved from http://www.innoviatech.com/insight/is-it-ethical-to-take-advantage-of-peoples-inherent-biases-four-principles-for-avoiding-the-misuse-of-behavioural-science-in-business/

Saghai, Y. (2013). The concept of nudge and its moral significance: A reply to Ashcroft, Bovens, Dworkin, WElch and Wertheimer. *Journal of Medical Ethics, 39*(8), 499–501.

Schwartz, B. (2004). *The paradox of choice: Why more is less*. New York: HarperCollins.

Sunstein, C. R. (2015a). *Nudging and choice architecture: Ethical considerations* (SSRN Scholarly Paper No. ID 2551264). Rochester, NY: Social Science Research Network. Retrieved from http://papers.ssrn.com/abstract=2551264

Sunstein, C. R. (2015b). *Why nudge?: The politics of libertarian paternalism* (Reprint ed.). New Haven, CT: Yale University Press.

Sunstein, C. R. (2016). *Do people like nudges?* (SSRN Scholarly Paper No. ID 2604084). Rochester, NY: Social Science Research Network. Retrieved from http://papers.ssrn.com/abstract=2604084

The Benefits of Applying Behavioural Science to Business

How to Get the Most Value from Behavioural Science

Abstract Chapter 9 is about the value of applying behavioural science in the private sector. It describes how managers in consumer-facing and business-to-business sectors can get value from its application, and how students of psychology and business can learn to apply behavioural theory to real-world problems. This chapter reprises the main themes of the book. First, if businesses apply the scientific method to understanding consumers and customers, they are more likely to know what is really driving behaviour, and hence be able to design products, services and interventions that better meet people's needs. Second, using a structured, evidence-based approach helps to navigate complexity and saves time and money in the long run. Finally, incorporating behavioural science into a commercial organisation can be highly beneficial if the company is clear about how it will add value and has a plan for how to introduce it.

Keywords Behaviour, drivers of • Consumer behaviour • Scientific method

We've seen that human behaviour is complex and hard to predict. We've covered the history of the discipline, why it's hard to predict behaviour, the theories and models that we use, and how we apply the theory to intervention design. We've looked at the application of behavioural science—how to integrate it into business, how to use it in multidisciplinary

© The Author(s) 2018
H. Rubinstein, *Applying Behavioural Science to the Private Sector*,
https://doi.org/10.1007/978-3-030-01698-2_9

teams, and what the potential pitfalls are to this approach. Let's see how this information might relate to you, and how it might affect your day-to-day work—whether you work in business or whether you are a student of business or psychology.

9.1   I Work in a Business that Sells Directly to Consumers. *How Can I Get the Most Value from Behavioural Science?*

If you work in a consumer-facing business, you will already be aware of the challenges to launching and selling products and services.

- People behave unpredictably and do not always do what they say they do
- New launches fail, or at least don't succeed as was hoped
- Efforts to predict behaviour often fail, frustrated by inaccuracies in the research and development process

Perhaps you'd previously heard about behavioural science and picked up this book to help you learn more about how you can actually use it. Often, consumer-facing businesses have had more exposure to behavioural science, and many are at the stage of wondering how to best integrate this new discipline. Wherever you are along your behavioural science journey, the information that you've learned from this book should help you see the next step that you need to take.

We have shown how the science of behaviour enables a deeper understanding of people's motivations, needs, and wants. It enables the design of better products and services—ones that people actually want, and that they find easy to understand and use.

The use of behavioural science in business can deliver substantial value. It can help in early-stage innovation, when developing radical communication strategies, for rethinking consumer experiences, or encouraging new ways of working in an organisation. The proper use of behavioural science can help your company stay ahead of the competition.

We discussed how existing market research approaches often fail, and this knowledge will help you to both better assess pre-existing data and to plan future research to be more effective. The intention–behaviour gap—the discrepancy between what people say and what they do—can be exacerbated by conventional research, which often yields poor-quality data, and which isn't properly analysed. The research design doesn't focus on the factors that actually drive behaviour, and often confirms existing biases because it aims to prove, and rarely seeks to refute, prior hypotheses. Research into products and services needs a better approach: one that will help to reduce the intention–behaviour gap. A programme that has a theoretical, scientific underpinning can help you to test your hypotheses with an open mind and to design your research programmes based around those factors that actually influence behaviour. This type of systematic approach to understanding human behaviour is more likely to accurately predict how people will respond to new products, services, processes, or communications, which should result in fewer market failures.

You may already be at the stage of deciding whether to employ a behavioural scientist. When selecting a behavioural scientist to help your business, you need someone who has actually had scientific training and experience in the area—preferably in the psychological and behavioural sciences. Without this training and experience, it is easy to make mistakes. For example, people may fail to understand the consequences of behaviour-change interventions that are not based in theory or evidence. There are many instances of these types of mistake, as the recent research into spill-over effects[1]—unforeseen consequences of behavioural interventions—has shown (Dolan & Galizzi, 2015; Xu & Schwarz, 2018).

It can be hard to integrate behavioural science into the company for reasons which can be emotional: the fear of disrupting current ways of working, the concern about the effectiveness and efficiency of the process, and the confusion about how this approach is different from other conventional approaches. This makes it easier for you to recognise these as barriers and to explicitly discuss, address, and minimise their impact.

There are, however, some ways to make the integration of a new behavioural science function easier. It is important to have a credible, experienced person to lead it. The team members you employ should have scientific training in a broad range of psychological and behavioural disciplines and you may want a fusion of different psychological disciplines, not a monolith of one. And even before you employ the team, you

---

[1] Spillovers occur because behaviours do not occur in isolation and 'spill over' to influence other behaviours. This can be good—'I exercised this morning, so I will eat more healthily' or bad—'I exercised this morning, so I can eat more chocolate'. Behaviour change always occurs within a specific context and if this is not fully understood there can be unintended (and sometimes negative) consequences.

need to plan its integration and seek internal champions. You will also need to develop a plan to introduce and promote it to as many people as possible to gain credibility within the company. And once the team is introduced, you might need to experiment to find an approach that fits with the organisation's existing culture, processes and values.

Behavioural science is best applied within a multidisciplinary team if the output is to have real-world relevance. Academics often talk about the benefits of cross-disciplinary working, but most universities are not set up to facilitate this. Businesses often know they should work in multidisciplinary teams, but the traditional business department structure makes this hard. Perhaps, if you're trying to introduce behavioural science, it's an ideal time to improve your capability for multidisciplinary working.

You might consider using behavioural science when:

- *commissioning market research*—consider going first to a behavioural scientist to check that the research will give you the information that you need
- *wondering how best to grow your company*—think about the potential value of introducing a behavioural scientist into your team
- *designing a breakthrough new product or service*—consider using behavioural science to work out what people desire and need, what drives their behaviour, and what would make it easy for them to engage with your product or service

9.2   I Work in a Business That Does Not Sell Directly to Consumers. How Can I Get the Most Value from Behavioural Science?

If you work in a business that sells products or services to other businesses, you have customers, not consumers. As you're not having to deal with the irrational, complicated public on a day-to-day business, you might not have considered how your business could use behavioural science. However, even if your customers are other businesses, you are still dealing with people. And your business will also have staff. Those staff are also people. So, how does this book directly apply to the work that you do?

Customers do not always appear to be making rational decisions, in part, because everyone is affected by biases, by assumptions, and by their pre-existing mental models. This book has not only shown why it's so hard to predict behaviour, but also has given you tools to help predict behaviour in a way that is more effective than simply using gut feel.

Understanding more about behavioural science can help to manage teams better, help to gain company buy-in, help to launch a new system or approach, and help to better meet the needs of business customers. You can still apply the scientific method to human behaviour problems, regardless of which human's behaviour you're trying to change! The principles are simple: understand the problem in context, define the intervention space, design interventions, select the best ones, and then test and evaluate them.

You might consider using behavioural science when:

- *designing a new service offering for your customers*—could a behavioural science approach make a difference?
- *assessing whether your offering meets what your customers need, and whether they are likely to buy it*
- *introducing a new way of working into the organisation*—can behavioural science be used to overcome resistance to change?

9.3   I'm a Student. How Can I Get the Most Value from Behavioural Science?

You're probably studying one of the psychological or behavioural sciences or you're studying business and management. Either way, you will have been exposed to a lot of theory, and you might be wondering how to apply this theory in the real world. It can be hard to see how to use this hard-earned knowledge to make a difference and to improve people's lives. This book has given you the tools to translate behavioural theory to intervention design. Often, this practical application is not well taught in university courses, and it's not familiar to businesses either. Until recently, it was used only in the health sector and in public policy, but it is now time for businesses to make more of this tool. In your future roles, you can help organisations to use it.

Often, when you're taught about theories and models, you don't learn how and why they are developed. Understanding this can help to explain the discrepancies between different approaches or the incongruities between different frameworks. It helps you to decide which models or theories you can apply in different situations.

You may well have been pondering your future career options. Perhaps you've considered working in a commercial organisation? Maybe you're concerned about the ethics of using behavioural science to change behaviour in a commercial context. People are often suspicious of the motives and drivers of large private organisations and are concerned that when these organisations have more power to influence their consumers' behaviour, that they might abuse this power. However, there is substantial debate about how to apply behavioural science in an ethical way. With the guidelines suggested, there is no reason that businesses can't use behavioural science in a way that benefits, rather than harming, their consumers. You don't have to compromise on your ethical principles.

Those studying business and management may be familiar with similar challenges to integrating new functions in a business. We have discussed the specific barriers to the introduction of behavioural science, and the techniques that can enable it. Many of these techniques can equally be applied to the integration of other business functions and considering the integration from a behavioural perspective can help you to develop a plan to make the process as smooth as possible.

You might consider using behavioural science when:

- revising for your exams: consider the practical situations that could benefit from the application of the theories and models that you're learning
- thinking about how theories and models are valuable for designing interventions to change behaviour in these situations

9.4   I INTERACT WITH OTHER HUMANS. *HOW CAN I GET THE MOST VALUE FROM BEHAVIOURAL SCIENCE?*

We all interact, regularly, with other humans in a personal or professional way. These humans can behave in ways that surprise or confuse you. You've heard many times in this book that it's hard to predict behaviour, but you now know that there's a better way to try to predict behaviour that is better than just guessing. You've got a new tool to help you understand why people don't always do what they say they do.

Behavioural science is a young and rapidly evolving field, and we are learning more and more about what is, or is not, effective at changing behaviour (French et al., 2012; Hardeman et al., 2002; Michie, West,

Sheals, & Godinho, 2018). We're also learning more and more about the potential risks.

At the time of writing, the global press has been discussing how a London-based consultancy, Cambridge Analytica, used data mining, data brokerage, and data analytics for strategic communication in elections. The data was based on psychological profiling to manipulate the information people received and hence, it is alleged, to bias elections. The ethical implications of the misuse of behavioural science are now in the public consciousness. People are concerned that this approach can be used to modify social norms and situations, in ways that they are unaware of, to manipulate them and limit their freedom of choice (Arneson, 2015; Glod, 2015; Raihani, 2013).

You know why you need to use this approach wisely, both from a moral and a reputational standpoint. The guidelines outlined in Chap. 8 give a way to assess the approaches that you choose. Businesses are faced with these dilemmas every day and having an objective way to assess these makes it easier to make the right decisions.

So, we've come to the end of this book. You should now understand why behavioural science provides a systematic, scientific way to understand the needs and motivations of consumers and employees and how you can use it to design products, services and processes that meet those needs.

Behavioural science is a powerful, new approach for understanding the needs and motivations of consumers and employees and for designing products, services and processes that meet those needs. Use it well.

References

Arneson, R. J. (2015). Nudge and shove. *Social Theory and Practice, 41*(4), 668–691. https://doi.org/10.5840/soctheorpract201541436

Dolan, P., & Galizzi, M. M. (2015). Like ripples on a pond: Behavioral spillovers and their implications for research and policy. *Journal of Economic Psychology, 47*, 1–16.

French, S. D., Green, S. E., O'Connor, D. A., McKenzie, J. E., Francis, J. J., Michie, S., … Grimshaw, J. M. (2012). Developing theory-informed behaviour change interventions to implement evidence into practice: A systematic approach using the Theoretical Domains Framework. *Implementation Science, 7*(1), 38. https://doi.org/10.1186/1748-5908-7-38

Glod, W. (2015). How nudges often fail to treat people according to their own preferences. *Social Theory and Practice, 41*(4), 599–617. https://doi.org/10.5840/soctheorpract201541433

Hardeman, W., Johnston, M., Johnston, D., Bonetti, D., Wareham, N., & Kinmonth, A. L. (2002). Application of the theory of planned behaviour in behaviour change interventions: A systematic review. *Psychology & Health,* *17*(2), 123–158. https://doi.org/10.1080/08870440290013644a

Michie, S., West, R., Sheals, K., & Godinho, C. A. (2018). Evaluating the effectiveness of behavior change techniques in health-related behavior: A scoping review of methods used. *Translational Behavioral Medicine,* *8*(2), 212–224. https://doi.org/10.1093/tbm/ibx019

Raihani, N. J. (2013). Nudge politics: Efficacy and ethics. *Frontiers in Psychology,* *4*, 1–3. https://doi.org/10.3389/fpsyg.2013.00972

Xu, A. J., & Schwarz, N. (2018). How one thing leads to another: Spillover effects of behavioral mind-sets. *Current Directions in Psychological Science,* *27*(1), 51–55. https://doi.org/10.1177/0963721417724238

Index[1]

[1] Note: Page numbers followed by 'n' refer to notes.

© The Author(s) 2018
H. Rubinstein, *Applying Behavioural Science to the Private Sector*,
https://Doi.org/10.1007/978-3-030-01698-2

CPSIA information can be obtained
at www.ICGtesting.com
Printed in the USA
LVHW020134261118
598238LV00012B/485/P